Guyanese Style Cooking

Guyanese Style Cooking

Bibi Sazieda Jabar

iUniverse, Inc.
Bloomington

Guyanese Style Cooking

iUniverse books may be ordered through booksellers or by contacting:

iUniverse
1663 Liberty Drive
Bloomington, IN 47403
www.iuniverse.com
1-800-Authors (1-800-288-4677)

ISBN: 978-1-4620-6336-9 (sc)
ISBN: 978-1-4620-6337-6 (ebk)

Printed in the United States of America

iUniverse rev. date: 01/23/2012

For Jonathan & Brandon
Forever Family!

AUTHOR'S EXPERIENCE AND BACKGROUND INFORAMTION

I learned to cook when I was barely seven years old and as I grew, cooking became more interesting and challenging to me. I soon discovered that cooking was my niche, because I was able to master Guyanese dishes, and enjoyed creating my own dishes. Experimenting with various ingredients, and revel at the amazing creations gave me such a rush! This is when I discovered that cooking was my passion! I developed a sense of pride with each dish and have continued to cook with pride and love. Every time I cook a dish my culinary skills improve because I challenge myself to make it better. Cooking and eating has become a very important part of me and my families' lives.

Guyana like most of the Caribbean countries has the most amazing and breathtaking sceneries just like their mouthwatering, lip smacking and finger licking culinary delights. Guyana has some of the most unique and flavorful dishes that you will ever taste. The ingredients and preparation of some of the traditional dishes are the most memorable, that I have learned from my grandparents. I am thrilled to share these traditional Guyanese dishes with a multi-cultural society who can truly appreciate a unique spicy Caribbean adventure!

You will notice throughout the book the scale for using "habanero pepper" is half for mild, one for medium and two for suicide heat. For those who are not accustomed to really spicy foods please DO NOT use any habanero. Guyanese enjoy a lot of heat in their dishes, which is why I used habanero in almost all of my dishes.

Preface v

Guyana is a small country in South America, between Surinam and Venezuela. The Capital is Georgetown and the population is approximately 765,283. Guyana is well-known for its naturally beautiful sceneries and majestic waterfalls. Where can someone appreciate the most spectacular scenic wonders while enjoying some of the tastiest cuisines? Guyana that is where!

Guyanese cuisine is unique but is closely related to the way most Caribbean dishes are prepared. There are a variety of foods in Guyana, such as boil & fry, curry, roti, cook-up and pepper pot. However, most traditional dishes consist of provisions which are grown in Guyana. Provisions are root vegetables such as cassava, plantain, eddoes, and tania. Cassavas and eddoes are considered substitutes for potatoes and tania is a relative of the yam. The Guyanese people are very creative because they create all kinds of by-products from these vegetables. For example, cassava is made into flour for roti and used in many other dishes.

A sauce called cassareep is made from the juice of cassava. It is boiled for a long time until it forms a brown and thick liquid called cassareep. Cassareep is used to make one of the most famous and traditional dishes in Guyana called *"Pepper Pot."* This dish is made with different types of meat, spices, and the most important ingredient is cassareep (*recipe on pages 24 & 30*). Pepper pot can be cooked with one type of meat or as many types as you desire. Cooking with cassareep adds a unique flavor and also helps preserve the dish for a number of days. For example, pepper pot does not have to be refrigerated, it can stay out for days and it will still be good to eat. The cassareep prevents it from going bad.

Another traditional dish is *"Boil & Fry"* which is a term used by Guyanese to refer to a popular way of cooking root vegetables. The root vegetables are also called *"ground provisions,"* which are easily grown in Guyana. This dish is prepared by peeling the provisions; boil them in salted water; drain and sauté with onion, tomatoes and fresh herbs *(recipe on page 41)*.

Guyana has an abundance of fish! Some of the sweetest fish I have ever tasted! One such fish is the *"Gilbaka,"* it is a meaty fish and is enjoyed by Guyanese *(recipe on page 54)*. The texture is firm and fleshy and there are no small bones to worry about. Another excellent fish is the *"Hassa."* It is black and covered with hard bones. Although, the hassa may look ugly and complicated to eat, it really is not. Once this fish is cooked the meat can be easily retrieved. It is also a very tasty fish *(recipe on page 56)*. In the western world you may know it by another name, "armored cat fish."

Gather your appetite and let's get started on this Guyanese culinary adventure!

Preface vi

CONTENTS

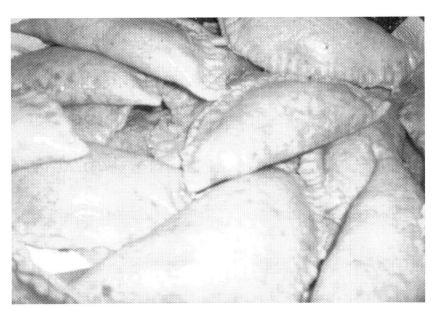

EASY PICNIC & PARTY SNACKS

BARA

1 cup yellow split peas 2 green onions, chopped
1 package quick rising yeast 1 tablespoon turmeric
2 cloves garlic Water
1 teaspoon parsley 2 cups cooking oil
Salt & black pepper to taste 1 medium onion, chopped
1 tablespoon baking powder 1 habanero pepper, chopped
2 cups all-purpose flour

STEPS:

1. Wash the split peas then soak in three cups of water overnight. Peas will expand overnight.

2. Next day, drain the water from the yellow split peas. Using a blender, add yellow split peas, fresh water (1/2 cup), onion, garlic, green onion, habanero and blend until mixture is smooth (no whole peas should remain). You may need to add some more water, *do not* make the mixture runny! Remove the mixture from blender, place into a large bowl and set aside.

3. Mix flour and baking powder together in a separate bowl, then add it into split peas mixture. Add black pepper, parsley, salt and turmeric into mixture and mix thoroughly.

4. Empty packet of yeast into two tablespoons of hot water and add it to the split peas/flour mixture. The consistency of the mixture should be firm *not* runny. Depending on how much water you added to blend the peas, you may or may not need to add more.

5. Cover mixed dough in the bowl with saran wrap. Set dough aside to rise for approximately 4 hours.

6. Heat cooking oil in a deep, medium sized pot (wok works best), on high heat; however, when oil is hot turn the heat down to medium.

7. Cut off pieces from mixture, flatten with palm and gently drop into hot oil (deep fry). Remove from oil when both sides are golden brown, place on serving dish. Ready to eat!

Serve: Hot or Cold
Portion: 25-30 pieces
Cooking time: 30 minutes, plus overnight preparation time
Best with: Chutney

CHUTNEY
1 medium tomato
2 tablespoons lemon juice or vinegar
1 habanero
1 medium onion
1 teaspoon salt
2 cloves garlic

STEP: Add all ingredients in a blender and blend until the consistency is smooth. Remove in a bowl and serve with bara.

Note: The amount of habanero pepper required may depend on the individual's preference.
½ habanero pepper = mild
1 habanero pepper = medium
2 habanero pepper = suicide

SPICY BEEF PATTIES
PASTRY
4 cups all-purpose flour

1 tablespoon turmeric

1/2 cup shortening (not melted)

1/2 cup margarine or butter (not melted)

1 teaspoon salt

3 eggs (2 for flour mixture & 1 for glazing)

FILLING
2 tablespoons cooking oil

Salt & black to taste

1 onion, chopped

3 pounds lean ground beef (ground turkey or chicken can be substituted)

2 tablespoons curry powder

2 habanero pepper (for extra spicy use more)

1 teaspoon dried thyme (fresh thyme preferable)

2 tablespoons tomato paste

1 cup fresh bread crumb

STEPS:
1. Mix flour, shortening, margarine, salt, turmeric and two eggs together. Add a quarter cup cold water and knead mixture until dough has a smooth consistency not sticky. Cover and set dough aside until filling is made.
2. Heat cooking oil in a large sized skillet, add the onion and cook until caramelized.
3. Add ground beef and cook for 10 minutes, breaking up chunks of meat with a spoon. Drain off excess fat if necessary.
4. Stir in all other ingredients and add one cup water; cover and cook for another 10 minutes. Set aside to cool.
5. Cut dough into small balls.
6. Using a rolling pin roll out ball of dough to form flat shell.
7. Add one tablespoon of beef mixture on rolled out pastry and fold over. Crimp edges with fork to seal.
8. Beat one egg thoroughly. Use a pastry brush to brush egg mixture over top of patties. Bake on greased cookie sheets at 325° F for 20 minutes or until golden brown. Spicy and delicious!

Serve: Hot or Cold
Portion: 20
Cooking time: 45 minutes
Best with: Chutney

Note: The amount of habanero pepper required may depend on the individual's preference.

½ habanero pepper = mild

1 habanero pepper = medium

2 habanero pepper = suicide

BHYGANI (EGG PLANT FRITTERS)

1 cup yellow split peas
1 medium egg plant
2 cloves garlic
1 teaspoon parsley (or fresh parsley)
1 teaspoon dried thyme (fresh thyme is best)
Salt & black pepper to taste
1 tablespoon baking powder
2 cups all-purpose flour
1 medium onion
2 green onions
1 tablespoon turmeric
Water
2 cups cooking oil
1 habanero pepper

STEPS:

1. Wash the split peas then soak in three cups of water overnight. Peas will expand overnight.

2. Next day, drain the water from the yellow split peas. Using a blender, add split peas, half cup of water, onion, garlic, green onion, habanero and blend until mixture is smooth (*no whole peas should remain*). You may need to add some more water, *do not* make the mixture runny! Remove the mixture from blender and place in a large bowl.

3. Mix flour and baking powder together in a separate bowl, then add it into blended split peas. Add black pepper, parsley, salt and turmeric into mixture and mix thoroughly.

4. Empty one packet of yeast into two tablespoons of hot water and add it to the split peas/flour mixture. The consistency of the mixture should be firm *not* runny. Depending on the how much water you added to blend the peas with, you may or may not need to add more.

5. Cover mixed dough in the bowl with saran wrap. Set dough aside to rise for 3 hours.

6. Wash & cut eggplant into thin slices and sprinkle with salt and pepper.

7. Make sure the oil is really hot before you turn it down to medium.

8. Using your hands or a spoon dip seasoned eggplant slices into batter and gently drop it into hot oil (*be sure eggplant piece is entirely covered with batter*).

10. Occasionally stir the bhyganis to make sure they are evenly cooked.

11. Once the bhyganis are golden brown use a spoon with holes to help drain off some of the oil before removing them from the pot. *I recommend you use paper towel to help soak up some of the oil.* Ready to serve and enjoy with chutney!

Serve: Hot or Cold
Portion: 25-30 pieces
Preparation time: 30 minutes, plus overnight preparation time
Best with: Chutney

CHUTNEY
1 medium tomato
2 tablespoons lemon juice or white vinegar
1 habanero
1 medium onion
1 teaspoon salt
2 cloves garlic
STEP: Add all ingredients in a blender and blend together until consistency is smooth. Remove in a bowl and serve with bhygani.

Note: The amount of habanero pepper required may depend on the individual's preference.
½ habanero pepper = mild
1 habanero pepper = medium
2 habanero pepper = suicide

BOILED CHICK PEAS (SOFT)

1-8 oz. package uncooked chick peas
Salt & black pepper to taste
½ habanero pepper, chopped
1 teaspoon parsley flakes (or fresh)
2 teaspoons tomato paste
1 medium onion, chopped
1 green onion, chopped
2 tablespoons cooking oil

STEPS:

1. Wash and soak the chick peas in large bowl with three cups of water overnight.

2. Next day, using a pressure cooker, add chick peas, two cups water (*water must be above chick peas in pressure cooker*), and cook for 20 minutes or if you have a timer on your pressure cooker until timer dings.

3. Remove the pressure cooker from the heat and let it cool down before opening it. Once it is opened check chick peas to ensure it is boiled the way you like.

4. Drain off the water by emptying the contents from the pressure cooker into a colander and set aside.

5. Heat cooking oil in a medium sized skillet (or wok), on medium heat, add the onion, green onion and cook until caramelized. Add chick peas, tomato paste, parsley, habanero, salt and black pepper.

6. Cook for five minutes and remove from heat. Read to eat!

Serve: Hot or Cold
Portion: 8-10
Cooking time: 30 minutes, plus overnight preparation time
Best with: Chutney, hot sauce or on its own

CHUTNEY
1 medium tomato
2 tablespoon lemon juice or white vinegar
1 habanero
1 medium onion
1 teaspoon salt
2 cloves garlic

STEP: Add all ingredients in a blender and blend until consistency is smooth. Remove in a bowl and serve with chick peas.

Note: The amount of habanero pepper required may depend on the individual's preference.
½ habanero pepper = mild
1 habanero pepper = medium
2 habanero pepper = suicide

BREADFRUIT CHIPS

1 breadfruit
Salt & black pepper to taste
2 tablespoons dried habanero pepper (crushed pepper)
2 cups cooking oil

STEPS:
1. Wash, peel and cut breadfruit into very thin slices.
2. Next, heat cooking oil in a frying pan (or wok), on medium heat.
3. Once the oil is hot gently drop in breadfruit slices and let cook until all sides are golden brown. For best results *do not* put all the breadfruit in at once. For one medium sized breadfruit, it will take at least three frying.
4. When frying is completed, sprinkle salt, black pepper, dried habanero and mix together. Ready to eat!

Serve: Hot or Cold
Cooking time: 20 minutes

Note: The amount of habanero pepper required may depend on the individual's preference.
½ habanero pepper = mild
1 habanero pepper = medium
2 habanero pepper = suicide

CASSAVA BALLS

1 cup yellow split peas
1 package frozen cassava
2 cloves garlic
1 teaspoon parsley (or fresh parsley)
1 teaspoon thyme (or fresh thyme)
Salt & black pepper to taste
1 tablespoon baking powder
2 cups all-purpose flour
2 green onions, chopped
1 medium onion, chopped
1 tablespoon turmeric
Water
2 cups cooking oil
1 habanero pepper

STEPS:

1. Wash the split peas then soak in three cups of water overnight. Peas will expand overnight.
2. Next day, drain the water from the yellow split peas. Using a blender, add split peas, half a cup of water, onion, garlic, green onion, habanero and blend until mixture is smooth (*no whole peas should remain*). You may need to add some more water, *do not* make the mixture runny. Remove the mixture from blender and place into a large bowl.
3. Mix flour and baking powder together in a separate bowl, then add it into blended split peas.
4. Add black pepper, parsley, salt and turmeric into mixture and mix thoroughly.
5. Empty one packet of yeast into two tablespoons of hot water and add it to the split peas/flour mixture. The consistency of the mixture should be firm *not* runny. Depending on the amount of water you added when the peas was blended, you may or may not need to add more.
6. Cover mixed dough in the bowl with saran wrap. Set dough aside to rise for 3 hours.
7. Peel and cube cassavas.
8. Boil cassava for 20 minutes or until it is soft enough to mash. When cassava is done drain water from the cassava using a colander.

9. Mash cassava and add salt and black pepper. Roll mashed cassava into balls.
10. Make sure the oil is really hot before you turn it down to medium.
11. Using your hands or a spoon dip cassava balls into batter and gently drop it into hot oil (*cassava balls should be fully covered with batter*).
12. Occasionally stir the cassava balls to make sure they are evenly cooked.
13. Once the cassava balls are golden brown use a spoon with holes to help drain off some of the oil before removing them from the pot. *I recommend you use paper towel to help soak up some of the oil.* Ready to serve and enjoy with chutney!

Serve: Hot or Cold
Portion: 25-30 pieces
Cooking time: 30 minutes, plus overnight preparation time
Best with: Chutney

CHUTNEY
1 medium tomato
2 tablespoon lemon juice or white vinegar
1 habanero
1 medium onion
1 teaspoon salt
2 cloves garlic

STEPS: Add all ingredients in blender and blend together until the consistency is smooth. Remove in a bowl and serve.
Note: The amount of habanero pepper required may depend on the individual's preference.
½ habanero pepper = mild
1 habanero pepper = medium
2 habanero pepper = suicide

EGG & CASSAVA BALLS

1 cup yellow split peas 1 tablespoon turmeric
6 hard-boiled eggs 2 cups cooking oil
3 medium cassavas 1 habanero pepper
2 cloves garlic Salt & black pepper to taste
1 teaspoon parsley 2 green onions, chopped
1 tablespoon baking powder 1 medium onion, chopped
2cups all-purpose flour

STEPS:

1. Wash the split peas then soak in three cups of water overnight. Peas will expand overnight.
2. Next day, drain the water from the yellow split peas. Using a blender, add split peas, half cup of water, onion, garlic, green onion, habanero and blend until mixture is smooth (no whole peas should remain). You may need to add some more water, *do not* make the mixture runny! Remove the mixture from blender and place into a large bowl.
3. Mix flour and baking powder together in a separate bowl, then add it into blended split peas.
4. Add black pepper, parsley, salt and turmeric into mixture and mix thoroughly.
5. Empty one packet of yeast into two tablespoons of hot water and add it to the split peas/flour mixture. The consistency of the mixture should be firm *not* runny. Depending on the how much water you added to blend the peas with, you may or may not need to add more.
6. Cover mixed dough in the bowl with saran wrap. Set dough aside to rise for 3 hours.
7. Peel and cube cassavas.
8. Boil cassava for 20 minutes or until it is soft enough to mash.
9. Boil the eggs in a separate pot for 10 minutes.
10. When the cassava is done, mash and add salt and black pepper.
11. When the eggs are done, peel and cut eggs into two (*lengthwise*) and cover with mashed cassava.
12. Make sure the oil is really hot before you turn it down to medium.
13. Using your hands or a spoon dip egg covered in cassava into batter and gently drop it into hot oil (*be sure egg is fully covered with batter*).

14. Occasionally stir the egg/cassava balls to make sure they are evenly cooked.

15. Once the egg/cassava balls are golden brown use a spoon with holes to help drain off some of the oil before removing them from the pot. *I recommend you use paper towel to help soak up some of the oil.* Ready to serve and enjoy with chutney!

Serve: Hot or Cold
Portion: 25-30 pieces
Best with: Chutney

CHUTNEY

1 medium tomato
2 tablespoon lemon juice or white vinegar
1 habanero
1 medium onion
1 teaspoon salt
2 cloves garlic

STEP: Add all ingredients in a blender and blend together until consistency is smooth. Remove in a bowl and serve with egg/cassava balls.

Note: The amount of habanero pepper required may depend on the individual's preference.
½ habanero pepper = mild
1 habanero pepper = medium
2 habanero pepper = suicide

FRIED CHICK PEAS (HARD)

1-8 oz. package uncooked chick peas
Salt & black pepper to taste
1 dried habanero pepper
2 cups cooking oil

STEPS:

1. Wash and soak uncooked chick peas in a large bow with three cups of water over night.
2. Next day, drain water and dry off chickpeas with paper towel (*let sit on flat pan to make sure chickpeas are completely dried*).
3. Heat oil in a deep, medium sized pot (or wok), on high heat. Once oil is hot add one third of chickpeas in and let it fry (*for best results, make sure oil is floating on top of chick peas*).
   Do not put all chick peas in at once, one package should take at least three times to fry.
4. Stir chick peas to ensure they are evenly cooked. Chick peas will be done when it is golden brown.
5. Using a spoon with holes to help drain off some of the oil while removing the chick peas from the pot. *I recommend you use paper towel to help soak up some of the oil.*
6. Place fried chick peas in a bowl and sprinkle with salt, black pepper and dried habanero pepper. Ready to eat!

Serve: Hot or ColdPortion: 8-10
Cooking time: 30 minutes, plus overnight preparation time
Best with: cold refreshing lime water (recipe on page 73)

Note: The amount of habanero pepper required may depend on the individual's preference.
½ habanero pepper = mild
1 habanero pepper = medium
2 habanero pepper = suicide

FRIED RIPE PLANTAIN

5 ripe plantains
2 tablespoon sugar
3 tablespoon cooking oil

STEPS:

1. Peel and cut plantain into halves then cut halves into long strips.
2. Add cooking oil into a medium sized frying pan (or wok), on high heat.
3. Oil must be really hot. Gently drop plantain into pan and deep fry until golden brown. *Do not* put all the plantain in at once. *Depending on the size of the frying pan, five plantains in a medium frying pan can take up to three frying.*
4. Occasionally stir plantains to ensure they are evenly cooked.
5. Using a spoon with holes drain most of the oil off before removing the plantains from the pot and place into a large platter.
6. Sprinkle sugar evenly over the top and serve.

Serve: Hot or Cold
Portion: 8-10
Cooking time: 15 minutes
Best with: vanilla ice cream

PHOLOURIE

1 cup yellow split peas
2 cloves garlic
1 teaspoon parsley flakes (or fresh parsley)
1 teaspoon dried thyme (or fresh thyme)
Salt & black pepper to taste
1 tablespoon baking powder
2 cups all-purpose flour
1 medium onion, chopped
2 green onions, chopped
1 tablespoon turmeric
Water
2 cups cooking oil
1 habanero pepper

STEPS:

1. Wash the split peas then soak in three cups of water overnight. Peas will expand overnight.
2. Next day, drain the water from the yellow split peas. Using a blender, add split peas, half cup of water, onion, garlic, green onion, habanero and blend until mixture is smooth (*no whole peas should remain*). You may need to add some more water, *do not* make the mixture runny. Remove the mixture from blender and place into a large bowl.
3. Mix flour and baking powder together in a separate bowl, then add it into blended split peas.
4. Add black pepper, parsley, salt and turmeric into mixture and mix thoroughly.
5. Empty one packet of yeast into two tablespoons of hot water and add it to the split peas/flour mixture. The consistency of the mixture should be firm *not* runny. Depending on the amount of water added when the peas was blended, you may or may not need to add more.
6. Cover mixed dough in the bowl with saran wrap. Set dough aside to rise for 3 hours.
7. Heat cooking oil in a deep, medium sized pot (or wok), on high heat.
8. Make sure the oil is really hot before you turn it down to medium.
9. Using your hands or a spoon cut off pieces of dough mixture and gently drop it into hot oil (deep fry).

10. Occasionally stir the pholouries to make sure they are evenly cooked.

11. Once the pholouries are golden brown use a spoon with holes to help drain off some of the oil before removing them from the pot. *I recommend you use paper towel to help soak up some of the oil.* Ready to serve!

Serve: Hot or Cold
Portion: 25-30 pieces
Cooking time: 30 minutes, plus overnight preparation time
Best with: Chutney

CHUTNEY

1 medium tomato
2 tablespoon lemon juice or white vinegar
1 habanero
1 medium onion
1 teaspoon salt
2 cloves garlic

STEPS: Add all ingredients in a blender and blend together until the consistency is smooth. Remove in a bowl and serve with pholourie.

Note: The amount of habanero pepper required may depend on the individual's preference.
½ habanero pepper = mild
1 habanero pepper = medium
2 habanero pepper = suicide

PLANTAIN CHIPS

5 green plantains
Salt & black pepper to taste
1 teaspoon dried habanero pepper
2 cups cooking oil

STEPS:

1. Peel plantains and thinly slice (see picture).
2. Heat cooking oil in a medium sized frying pan (or wok), on medium heat.
3. Oil needs to be really hot, but once the oil is hot, turn the heat to medium.
4. Next, gently add plantain to hot oil and cook until golden brown. *For best results do not put all the plantains in at once; five plantains will take at least three frying.*
5. Occasionally stir plantains to ensure they are evenly cooked.
6. Using a spoon with holes drain most of the oil off before removing the plantains from the pot and place into a good size bowl.
7. Add salt, black pepper, dried habanero and mix together. Ready to serve!

Serve: Hot or Cold
Portion: 10
Cooking time: 25 minutes
Best with: ginger beer (recipe on page 72)

Note: The amount of habanero pepper required may depend on the individual's preference.

½ habanero pepper = mild

1 habanero pepper = medium

2 habanero pepper = suicide

POTATO BALLS

1 cup yellow split peas 5-6 medium potatoes
1 teaspoon parsley (or fresh parsley) 2 cloves garlic
1 teaspoon dried thyme (or fresh thyme) Salt & black pepper to taste
1 tablespoon baking powder 1 medium onion, chopped
2 cups all-purpose flour 2 green onions, chopped
1 tablespoon turmeric 1 habanero pepper
Water 2 cups cooking oil

STEPS:

1. Wash the split peas then soak in three cups of water overnight. Peas will expand overnight.
2. Next day, drain the water from the yellow split peas. In a blender, add split peas, half cup water, onion, garlic, green onion, habanero and blend until mixture is smooth (*no whole peas should remain*). You may need to add some more water, *do not* make the mixture runny. Remove the mixture from the blender and place into a large bowl.
3. Mix flour and baking powder together in a separate bowl, and then mix in with blended split peas.
4. Add black pepper, parsley, salt and turmeric into mixture and mix thoroughly.
5. Empty one packet of yeast into two tablespoons of hot water and add it to the split peas/flour mixture. The consistency of the mixture should be firm *not* runny. Depending on the amount of water added when peas were blended, you may or may not need to add more.
6. Cover mixed dough in the bowl with saran wrap. Set dough aside to rise for 3 hours.
7. Peel, quarter potatoes and boil for 20 minutes.
8. Drain potatoes using a colander.
9. Mash potatoes, add salt and black pepper. Let cool and roll potatoes into balls.
10. Heat cooking oil in a deep, medium sized pot (or wok), on high heat. Oil needs to be very hot before turning down heat to medium.
11. Using your hands or spoon dip potato balls into batter (*ensure potato is fully covered with batter*), and gently drop into hot oil (deep fry).
12. Occasionally stir the potato balls to ensure they are evenly cooked.

13. Once the potato balls are golden brown use a spoon with holes to help drain off some of the oil before removing them from the pot. *I recommend you use paper towel to help soak up some of the oil.* Ready to serve!

Serve: Hot or Cold
Portion: 25-30 pieces
Cooking time: 30 minutes, plus overnight preparation time
Best with: Chutney

CHUTNEY

1 medium tomato
2 tablespoon lemon juice or white vinegar
1 habanero
1 medium onion
1 teaspoon salt
2 cloves garlic

STEPS: Add all ingredients in a blender and blend together until the consistency is smooth. Remove in a bowl and serve with potato balls.

Note: The amount of habanero pepper required may depend on the individual's preference.
½ habanero pepper = mild
1 habanero pepper = medium
2 habanero pepper = suicide

STUFFED POTATOES

4 medium potatoes
½ cup cottage cheese
½ cup grated cheddar cheese
¼ cup butter
Salt& black pepper to taste
½ habanero pepper, chopped

DIRECTIONS:

1. Set oven to 325° F.
2. Wash potatoes and bake for approximately 20 minutes.
3. Split the potatoes into two and scoop out the insides.
4. Mash in a bowl with cottage cheese, cheddar cheese, butter, salt, black pepper and habanero.
5. Spoon the mixture back into the shells, filling the shells to the top. Place on baking sheet.
6. Approximately 15 minutes before you are ready to eat, put the potatoes back into the oven and bake until heated through and very light brown.

Serve: Hot
Portion: 4
Cooking time: 40 minutes
Best with: any meat or by itself

Note: The amount of habanero pepper required may depend on the individual's preference.
½ habanero pepper = mild
** 1 habanero pepper = medium**
** 2 habanero pepper = suicide**

TUNA/COD FISH CAKES

1-8oz can tuna fish or cod fish

2 eggs

5-6 medium potatoes, boiled

2 cloves garlic

1 teaspoon parsley flakes (or fresh parsley)

1 teaspoon thyme (or fresh thyme)

1 green onion, chopped

Salt & black pepper to taste

3 tablespoon cooking oil

1 habanero pepper, chopped

STEPS:

1. Peel, quarter potatoes and boil for 15 minutes.
2. Drain potatoes using a colander.
3. Mash potatoes; add tuna or cod fish, habanero, green onion, salt and black pepper.
4. Roll potato mixture into balls then flatten into cakes.
5. Beat eggs with a dash of salt and black pepper.
6. Heat cooking oil in a medium sized frying pan, on high heat; however, when oil is hot turn heat down to medium.
7. Dip potato/tuna/cod fish cakes into egg batter and fry until both sides are golden brown.
8. Remove from pan and place on a platter. Ready to serve!

Serve: Hot or Cold
Portion: 10
Cooking time: 20 minutes
Best with: Chutney

CHUTNEY

1 medium tomato

2 tablespoon lemon juice or white vinegar

1 habanero

1 medium onion

1 teaspoon salt

2 cloves garlic

STEP: Add all ingredients in a blender and blend together until the consistency is smooth. Remove in a bowl and serve with tuna/cod fish cakes.

Note: The amount of habanero pepper required may depend on the individual's preference.
½ **habanero pepper = mild**
1 **habanero pepper = medium**
2 **habanero pepper = suicide**

Beef-Barley

SCRUMPTIOUS SOUPS

BEEF & BARLEY WITH DUMPLINGS

1 lb. stewing beef

1 medium onion, chopped

2 medium carrots (vegetables may be substituted with cassava & plantains)

3 cups water (beef stock can be substituted)

2 medium potatoes

½ cup barley

1 green onion, chopped

1 cup all-purpose flour

1 tablespoon baking powder

Salt & pepper to taste

1 teaspoon parsley flakes (or fresh parsley)

1 teaspoon dried thyme (or fresh thyme)

½ habanero pepper, chopped

STEPS:

1. In a medium sized bowl combine flour and baking powder together. Add water and knead until mixture forms into dough and set aside.
2. Wash barley and boil in a deep pot with two cups of water or beef stock. Let boil on medium heat until barley is tender, approximately 25 minutes.
3. Heat cooking oil in a medium sized frying pan.
4. Add chopped onion, green onion and cook until caramelized. Turn heat to medium.
5. Add stewing beef, parsley, thyme, salt, black pepper, habanero pepper and cook for 10 minutes.
6. Add partially cooked stewing beef, onion, and green onion into the pot with barley.
7. Peel potatoes and carrots, cut into cubes and add to barley. If desired add more water and cook for approximately 15 minutes or until the vegetables are cooked to your satisfaction. *Remember if you used cassavas and plantains as substitutes, it may require more than 15 minutes to cook.*
8. Using the dough that was prepared at the beginning, divide dough into small balls and add to soup.
9. Cover and cook for an additional five minutes or until the dumplings are fully cooked. Ready to eat!

Serve: Hot or Cold
Portion: 6-8 people
Cooking time: 60 minutes
Best with: hot sauce

Note: The amount of habanero pepper required may depend on the individual's preference.
½ habanero pepper = mild
1 habanero pepper = medium
2 habanero pepper = suicide

CHICKEN & DUMPLINGS

1 chicken breast, cubed

1 medium onion, chopped

1 cup yellow split peas

2 medium cassavas (fresh or frozen)

2 green plantains

3 cups water (chicken stock can be substituted)

2 medium sweet potatoes

1 green onion

1 cup all-purpose flour

1 tablespoon baking powder

Salt & pepper to taste

1 teaspoon parsley flakes (or fresh)

1 habanero pepper, chopped

STEPS:

1. Combine flour and baking powder in a medium sized bowl. Add water and knead until mixture forms into dough and set aside.
2. Wash split peas and boil in stock pot with two cups of water or chicken stock. Cook on medium until peas are boiled, approximately 25 minutes or continue to boil the peas as you like.
3. Heat cooking oil in a medium sized frying pan; add the onion, green onion and cook until caramelized.
4. Add chicken, parsley, salt, black pepper, habanero and cook for 10 minutes.
5. Add cooked chicken into the pot with split peas.
6. Peel sweet potatoes, cassavas, plantains, cut into small pieces and add into the pot. Cook for another 20 minutes or until the vegetables are cooked to your satisfaction. *You may need to add more water in order for vegetable to cook fully.*
7. Using the dough that you mixed in the beginning, divide dough into small balls and add to soup.
8. Cover and cook for an additional five minutes or until the dumplings are fully cooked. Ready to eat!

Serve: Hot or Cold
Portion: 6-8 people
Cooking time: 60 minutes
Best with: hot pepper

Note: The amount of habanero pepper required may depend on the individual's preference.

½ habanero pepper = mild

1 habanero pepper = medium

2 habanero pepper = suicide

CHICKEN NOODLE

1 chicken breast, cubed
1 medium onion, chopped
2 medium carrots
3 cups water (chicken stock can be substituted or you can use a combination)
2 medium potatoes
1 green onion, chopped
Salt & black pepper to taste
1 teaspoon parsley flakes (or fresh)
½ package wide egg noodles (other noodles can be substituted)
½ habanero pepper, chopped

STEPS:

1. In a medium sized pot boil water or chicken stock on high heat and add noodles.
2. Peel and quarter potatoes and carrots.
3. Add into the boiling water or chicken stock.
4. Heat cooking oil in a medium sized frying; add the onion, green onion, habanero and cook until caramelized.
5. Add chicken, vegetables, black pepper, salt, and parsley flakes.
6. Add partially cooked chicken into the pot.
7. Cook for approximately 25 minutes on medium heat or until vegetables are cooked to your satisfaction. Enjoy soup with crackers or by itself!

Serve: Hot or Cold
Portion: 6-8 people
Cooking time: 40 minutes
Best with: Hot sauce

Note: The amount of habanero pepper required may depend on the individual's preference.
½ habanero pepper = mild
1 habanero pepper = medium
2 habanero pepper = suicide

CHICKEN & VEGETABLE

1 chicken breast, cubed
1 medium tomato, chopped
1 tablespoon tomato paste
1 medium onion, chopped
2 medium carrots
2 celery stalks
4 cups water (chicken stock can be substituted)
2 medium potatoes
1 green onion, chopped
Salt & black pepper to taste
1 teaspoon parsley flakes (or fresh)
1 teaspoon dried thyme (or fresh thyme)
2 tablespoons cooking oil
¼ cup shell noodles (other noodles may be substituted)
½ habanero pepper, chopped

STEPS:

1. In a deep, medium sized pot boil four cups of water or chicken stock on high heat. If you choose to use water, salt and pepper to taste.
2. Peel and cubed potatoes and carrots; cut celery stalks into cubes and add into pot.
3. Heat cooking oil in a medium sized frying pan; add the onion, green onion, habanero and cook until caramelized.
4. Add cubed chicken breast, black pepper, salt, parsley flakes, thyme, and tomato paste into frying pan and cook for approximately 15 minutes on medium heat.
5. Add contents of frying pan into pot with water and cook for 20 minutes or until vegetable are cooked to your satisfaction. *Please note that tomatoes should be added after 10 minute, do not add it sooner.*
6. Add noodles if desired and let it cook for another 15 minutes. *This soup will keep you warm on those cold winter days!*

Serve: Hot or Cold
Portion: 6-8 people
Cooking time: 40 minutes
Best with: Hot sauce

Note: The amount of habanero pepper required may depend on the individual's preference.

½ habanero pepper = mild

🌶 1 habanero pepper = medium

🌶🌶2 habanero pepper = suicide

YELLOW SPLIT PEA (DAHL SOUP)

1 pound stewing beef
½ cup yellow split peas
1 medium onion, chopped
2 green plantains
2 medium cassavas
3-4 eddoes (optional)
2 medium sweet potatoes
3 cups water
1 green onion, chopped
1 cup all-purpose flour
1 teaspoon baking powder
Salt & black pepper to taste
1 teaspoon parsley flakes (or fresh)
1 teaspoon dried thyme (or fresh)
1 habanero pepper, chopped

STEPS:

1. Combine flour and baking powder in a medium sized bowl. Add water and knead until mixture forms into dough and set aside.

2. Add two cups of water and split peas into a pressure cooker. Cook on high heat for approximately 15 minutes. *The split peas can be cooked in a medium sized pot for 30 minutes on medium heat or until peas are boiled.*

3. Remove pressure cooker from stove and run under cold water or until steam has evaporated.

4. Carefully open pressure cooker and place opened pressure cooker back onto stove on medium heat. *If you used a pot, continue to boil peas on medium heat.*

5. Add one cup of water, salt and pepper to taste and let this cook slowly.

6. Heat cooking oil in a medium sized frying pan; add the onion, green onion and cook until caramelized.

7. Add stewing beef, parsley, thyme, salt, black pepper, habanero and cook for 10 minutes.

8. Add partially cooked beef into the pressure cooker or pot with split peas.

9. Peel and cut plantains, eddoes, sweet potatoes, cassavas and add into the pressure cooker or pot. *Additional water may be needed.* Cook on medium heat for another 20 minutes, or until the vegetables are cooked as you desire.

10. Divide dough into small balls and add into the pressure cooker or pot.

11. Cover the pressure cooker or pot and cook for an additional five minutes. Turn off the stove and enjoy this delicious soup!

Serve: Hot or Cold
Portion: 6-8 people
Cooking time: 40 minutes
Best with: hot pepper

Note: The amount of habanero pepper required may depend on the individual's preference.
½ habanero pepper = mild
1 habanero pepper = medium
2 habanero pepper = suicide

Chicken, Broccoli & Rice

ENTICING ENTREES

ALFREDO SPICY PASTA & SHRIMP

1-1 lb. box bow tie pasta (any pasta can be used)

1 pound peeled shrimp (may be substitute for chicken or beef)

1-8 oz. Jar Ragu Classic Alfredo Sauce (any sauce can be used)

¼ cup butter

Salt & black pepper to taste

1medium onion, chopped

1 green onion, finely chopped

3 tablespoons olive oil

1 teaspoon parsley flakes (or fresh)

1 teaspoon oregano flakes (or fresh)

½ habanero pepper, chopped

Parmesan cheese

STEPS:

1. In large sized pot, add three cups of water, pasta a pinch of salt and one tablespoon of olive oil. Cook for approximately 20 minutes on medium heat.
2. Drain pasta using a colander. While pasta is draining in colander add butter and season with parsley, oregano and black pepper
3. Heat the remaining olive oil in a medium sized pot, on high heat.
4. Add the onion and green onion and cook until caramelized.
5. Add shrimp and turn heat to low so shrimp is not overcooked.
6. Add the pasta & alfredo sauce to the pot with the shrimp and continue to cook on low heat for five minutes.
7. Sprinkle parmesan cheese on top before serving. *The habanero is just enough in this dish to give it that "kick" Bon-appetite!*

Serve: Hot
Portion: 4-6
Cooking time: 25 minutes
Best with: any meat or by itself

Note: The amount of habanero pepper required may depend on the individual's preference.
½ habanero pepper = mild
1 habanero pepper = medium
2 habanero pepper = suicide

BAKE & SALTFISH

3 cups all-purpose flour

2 tablespoons baking powder

2 cups of cooking oil

1 cup water

1 pound salted cod fish

1 medium tomato

Salt is not recommended since the cod fish will have ample salt

1 teaspoon black pepper

1 teaspoon parsley flakes (or fresh)

1 teaspoon dried thyme (or fresh)

1 teaspoon oregano flakes (or fresh)

1 medium onion, chopped

1 green onion, chopped

1 habanero pepper, chopped

STEPS:

1. Combine flour and baking powder in a medium sized bowl and knead into dough. Set aside for 30 minutes.
2. Roll dough into three balls, roll out (one at a time) with a rolling pin (use a flat surface).
3. Cut rolled out dough into four pieces with butter knife.
4. *It is best to use a deep pot to deep fry the bake.* Heat oil in deep, medium sized pot (or wok), turn heat to medium. Carefully drop flat cut dough pieces in hot oil.
5. Occasionally stir to ensure bakes are evenly cooked. *This should take approximately one minute to cook.*
6. Use a spoon with holes to help drain off some of the oil while removing the bakes from the pot. *I recommend you use paper towel to help soak up some of the oil.*
7. Place bakes in a flat platter. Ready to serve with salted cod fish.
8. In a small sized pot, add one cup of water and boil salted cod.
9. Drain salted cod using a colander. Let the salted cod cool down before cutting it into pieces.
10. Heat cooking oil in a medium sized frying pan. Add the onion, green onion, habanero and cook until caramelized.
11. Add cod, season with spices and cook until golden brown. *Now you are ready to enjoy this traditional Guyanese dish with bake (above)!*

Serve: Hot or Cold
Portion: 6-8 people
Cooking time: 30 minutes
Best with: Chutney

CHUTNEY
1 medium tomato
1 habanero
¼ teaspoon salt
3 cloves garlic (minced)
½ onion, chopped

STEPS: Add all ingredients in a blender and blend together until the consistency is smooth. Remove in a bowl and serve with meal.

Note: The amount of habanero pepper required may depend on the individual's preference.
½ habanero pepper = mild
1 habanero pepper = medium
2 habanero pepper = suicide

BEEF IN BEER

3 lbs. piece of beef (round, blade or cross rib cut 2 inch thick)
1-2 oz. beer (any kind will do)
½ cup cooking oil
2 tablespoons vinegar
2 tablespoons brown sugar
1 medium onion, chopped
2 cloves garlic, crushed
1 teaspoon thyme (fresh thyme is best)
Salt & black pepper to taste
1 habanero pepper, chopped

STEPS:

1. With a metal skewer or barbecue fork poke holes all in the meat. This will allow the marinade to really soak in.

2. Put meat into a large zip-lock plastic bag, add all the ingredients, squishing bag with your hands to mix everything evenly into the meat. Press air out of the bag and zip the bag closed. Refrigerate for at least eight hours or for best results I recommend overnight.

3. Next day, fire up the grill, cook meat over high heat for a couple of minutes on each side. Save the marinade to use later. Turn grill down to medium and continue cooking over medium heat for approximately 40 minutes or until the meat is cooked to your preference. *If you are not sure, cut meat near the center to check.*

4. In a medium sized pot boil the remaining beer marinade that you saved for 10 minutes. Slice meat thinly on an angle and serve the sauce. Ready to eat!

Serve: Hot
Portion: 4-6 people
Cooking time: 60 minutes, plus overnight preparation time
Best with: Potatoes and vegetables

Note: The amount of habanero pepper required may depend on the individual's preference.
½ habanero pepper = mild
1 habanero pepper = medium
2 habanero pepper = suicide

BEEF & BROCCOLI STIR FRY

2 tablespoons cornstarch
1 tablespoon soya sauce
2 tablespoons cooking oil
2 cloves garlic, minced
4 cups broccoli (or 1 bunch)
1-10 oz. can condense consommé
1 lb. boneless beef sirloin or steak (cut into strips)
1 medium onion, sliced
Cooked rice or noodles
½ habanero pepper, chopped

STEPS:

1. In a small bowl stir together cornstarch, consommé and soya sauce and set aside.
2. Heat half of cooking oil in a medium sized frying pan and stir-fry beef with garlic until brown. Remove beef from frying pan and set aside.
3. Reduce heat. Using the same frying pan, add remaining oil, and stir-fry the broccoli, onion, and habanero until caramelized.
4. Add cornstarch mixture and cook until thickens, stirring constantly.
5. Add reserved beef to frying pan, and simmer for five minutes. Ready to serve!

Serve: Hot or Cold
Portion: 4-6
Cooking time: 20 minutes
Best with: Rice or noodles

Note: The amount of habanero pepper required may depend on the individual's preference.
½ habanero pepper = mild
1 habanero pepper = medium
2 habanero pepper = suicide

BEEF PEPPER POT

2 lbs. stewing beef
1 medium onion, chopped
2 cloves garlic, minced
2 habanero peppers, chopped
2 tablespoons cooking oil
3 tablespoons sugar
6 tablespoons casareep
1 teaspoon dried thyme (fresh thyme is best)
1 teaspoon parsley (or fresh)

STEPS:

1. Using a medium sized pressure cooker, add two cups of water, beef, salt and black pepper and pressure cook for 10 minutes and set aside. *Beef can be boiled but it will take longer approximately 30 minutes.*
2. Heat cooking oil in a medium sized frying pan, add the onion, garlic and habanero and cook for three minutes, or until caramelized.
3. While the above are cooking, remove the lid from the pressure cooker and put it back on the stove (without the lid), on medium heat. *Beef should be nicely submerged in the liquid, if there is not enough water add half cup of water.*
4. Add contents from frying pan to the pressure cooker and cook for 20 minutes.
5. Add sugar, casareep, thyme, parsley and continue to cook on medium heat.
6. Let this cook on low/medium heat for another 30 minutes. *Stew should be fairly thick and dark in color; if not dark enough add more casareep.*

This is probably the most famous, traditional Guyanese dish made with Casareep. The native people of Guyana boil fresh cassava juice to make fresh casareep for this dish. But since we are in the western world we have to settle for store bought casareep. Although it is not freshly made it is very close to the real thing!

This dish is better if it is cooked slowly for at least two hours. You may want to consider using a crock pot instead of a pressure cooker or a regular pot. I would recommend it because the meat will be even tenderer and once all the ingredients are in the crock pot you can forget about it for two hours. **The spicier this dish is the better it will taste!**

Serve: Hot
Portion: 6-8 people
Cooking time: 60 minutes or depending on your preference
Best with: Bread or by itself

Note: The amount of habanero pepper required may depend on the individual's preference.

½ **habanero pepper = mild**
 1 habanero pepper = medium
2 habanero pepper = suicide

BEEF STROGANOFF

1 lb. boneless beef (inside round or sirloin steak)
1-8 oz. can condense cream of mushroom soup
4 cups cooked noodles/rice
2 tablespoons margarine/butter
1 medium onion, chopped
1 teaspoon paprika
½ cup sour cream
1 teaspoon parsley flakes (or fresh)
1 teaspoon dried thyme (or fresh)
Salt & pepper to taste
1 habanero pepper, chopped

STEPS:

1. Follow package directions to cook noodles or rice and set aside.
2. Slice beef into thin strips. *For easier slicing I suggest you cut the beef across the grain.*
3. Add margarine/butter in a large sized pot (or wok) and cook over high heat.
4. Add the beef and onion until meat is no longer pink.
5. Add condensed soup, paprika, thyme and parsley; and cook for 15 minutes, stirring occasionally.
6. Remove from heat and stir in sour cream and place on a bed of noodles or rice. Enjoy!

Serve: Hot
Portion: 4-6 people
Cooking time: 40 minutes
Best with: Noodles or Rice

Note: The amount of habanero pepper required may depend on the individual's preference.
½ habanero pepper = mild
1 habanero pepper = medium
2 habanero pepper = suicide

CHICKEN/BROCCOLI & RICE

6 chicken breasts, cubed

1 cup milk

2 cups fresh or frozen broccoli

2 tablespoons margarine/butter

1 can condense cream of broccoli soup

1 cup sliced carrots

1-½ cups, uncooked quick-cooking rice

Salt & pepper to taste

1 habanero pepper, chopped

STEPS:

1. In large sized pot (or wok) over medium heat melt margarine/butter.
2. Add chicken and brown all sides, remove from heat and set aside. *Pour off fat if necessary.*
3. Using the same pot, add condense cream soup, milk and habanero. Return chicken to pot, bring to a boil, reduce heat to low, cover and simmer for 15 minutes.
4. While the chicken is cooking, wash the rice in a medium sized bowl and set it aside.
5. Add broccoli and carrots to the pot, and let it cook for five minutes.
6 Add the rice, stir then cover the pot and slowly cook until the rice is done the way you like.
7. Let stand five minutes and fluff with fork before serving.

I learned to cook this dish from by oldest brother, Fazil. However, I had to experiment with it and add my own special touches, before it became "my" creation. This is not a typical Guyanese dish, if anything it has more of an "American" flavor to it, but when the "habanero" is added it quickly gives it that unique Guyanese flavor. You might say that, "everything is better with habanero" for Guyanese!

Serve: Hot
Portion: 4-6
Cooking time:
Best with: Potatoes and vegetables

Note: The amount of habanero pepper required may depend on the individual's preference.

½ habanero pepper = mild

1 habanero pepper = medium

2 habanero pepper = suicide

CHICKEN & MUSHROOM SAUTE

2 tablespoons margarine/butter
1 lb. chicken breast, cubed
2 cups sliced mushrooms
1 medium onion, chopped
1 can condense cream of mushroom soup
½ cup milk
Tomatoes and chopped parsley for garnish
Salt & pepper to taste
1 habanero pepper, chopped

STEPS:

1. In a large pot (or wok) over medium heat, melt half of the margarine/butter.
2. Add chicken, salt and black pepper and cook for approximately five minutes. Remove from the pot and set aside.
3. In same pot melt remaining margarine/butter; sauté mushrooms, habanero and onion until caramelized.
4. Stir in the condensed soup and milk and bring to a boil.
5. Add the reserved chicken to the pot; let it simmer for five minutes. *Garnish with tomatoes and parsley. Enjoy this delicious spicy creation!*

Serve: Hot
Portion: 4-6
Cooking time: 20 minutes
Best with: Noodles or rice

Note: The amount of habanero pepper required may depend on the individual's preference.
½ habanero pepper = mild
1 habanero pepper = medium
2 habanero pepper = suicide

CHILI GUYANESE STYLE

2-8 oz. cans kidney beans

2 lb. group beef (ground chicken & turkey can be substituted)

1 medium onion, chopped

1-8 oz. can mushrooms

2-8 oz. cans tomato sauce

1-8 oz. can stew tomatoes

Salt & pepper to taste

2 habanero pepper, chopped

SAUCE MIX

3 tablespoons water

1 tablespoon all-purpose flour

2 teaspoons chili powder

STEPS:

1. In a deep medium sized pot brown ground beef. Drain off excess fat if necessary.
2. Add onion, habanero and cook until onion is caramelized.
3. Add kidney beans, mushrooms, tomato sauce, stewed tomatoes and cook on medium heat for 10 minutes.
4. Add the sauce mix (water, all-purpose flour and chili powder).
5. Cover pot half way and continue to simmer on medium heat for 40 minutes, stirring occasionally. *This dish can be cooked in a crock pot. The same steps can be used, except instead of using a pot substitute with the crock pot.*

My children have tried many different types of chilies but they always come back for mine; they say that my chili is simply the tastiest, with the perfect amount of heat. **However, it you prefer your chili extra spicy add at least two habaneros.**

Serve: Hot or Cold
Portion: 6-8 people
Cooking time: 45 minutes
Best with: Bread or plain

Note: The amount of habanero pepper required may depend on the individual's preference.

½ habanero pepper = mild

🌶 1 habanero pepper = medium

🌶🌶2 habanero pepper = suicide

CHOW MEIN (NOODLES)

1 package Guyanese style Chow Mein (noodles)
Salt & black pepper to taste
1 tablespoon butter/margarine
1 teaspoon accent salt
1 teaspoon tomato paste
1 teaspoon parsley flakes (or fresh)
1 teaspoon dried thyme (or fresh)
1 medium onion, chopped
1 green onion, chopped
2 tablespoons cooking oil
¼ cup frozen mixed vegetables
1 lb. boneless chicken breast (other meat can be substituted)
1 habanero pepper, chopped

DIRECTIONS:

1. In a deep medium sized pot, boil Chow Mein for approximately 15 minutes on medium heat.
2. Add mixed vegetables for the last two minutes then drain using a colander.
3. Make sure the Chow Mein is completely drained before adding margarine/butter and vegetables and set aside.
4. Using the same pot heat cooking oil on medium heat; add the onion, green onion, habanero and cook until caramelized.
5. Add chicken, tomato paste, salt, black pepper, parsley, thyme and accent and cook on medium heat until chicken is tender (*should be approximately 10 minutes).*
6. Add reserved Chow Mein and vegetables in the pot and thoroughly stir.
7. Let cool for five minute and serve.

Enjoying Guyanese style Chow Mein is very simple; the most difficult part of this dish will be to locate the noodles. But even that does not pose as a problem, since there is at least one West Indian grocery store on every street corner in the United States and especially in Canada. Of course if you live in Ocala, that might be another story!

Serve: Hot or Cold
Portion: 6-8 people
Cooking time: 25 minutes
Best with: Chutney

CHUTNEY
1 medium tomato
1 habanero
1 teaspoon salt
½ medium onion
2 cloves garlic

STEP: Add all ingredients in a blender and blend until the consistency is smooth. Remove in a bowl and serve with Chow Mein.

Note: The amount of habanero pepper required may depend on the individual's preference.
½ habanero pepper = mild
1 habanero pepper = medium
2 habanero pepper = suicide

COW FOOT PEPPER POT (STEW)

1 cow foot (clean and cut into pieces)
1 lb. stewing beef
½ cup white vinegar
1 medium onion, chopped
2 cloves garlic, minced
2 tablespoons cooking oil
3 tablespoons sugar
6 tablespoons casareep
1 teaspoon thyme (fresh thyme is best)
1 teaspoon parsley flakes (fresh is best)
Salt & pepper to taste
2 habanero peppers, chopped

STEPS:

1. Make sure cow foot is clean (remove any hairs) and thoroughly wash with white vinegar.
2. Using a pressure cooker, add three cups of water, beef, cow foot, salt and black pepper and pressure cook on medium heat for approximately 20 minutes and set aside. *A pot can be used to boil the cow foot and beef but it will take a longer time to cook, approximately 40 minutes.*
3. Heat cooking oil in a medium sized frying pan; add the onion, garlic, habanero pepper and cook until caramelized.
4. Remove the lid from the pressure cooker and place pressure cooker back onto stove on medium heat (*do not cover the pressure cooker*).
5. Add the contents from the frying pan in the pressure cooker with the beef and cow foot.
6. Add sugar, casareep, thyme, parsley and let it simmer on medium heat.
7. Cook on low/medium heat for approximately 60 minutes (*do not pressure*). Stew should be fairly thick and dark in color, if it is not add more casareep.

This dish is better if it is cooked slowly for at least two hours. You may want to consider using a crock pot instead of a pressure cooker or a regular pot. I would recommend it because the meat will be even tenderer and once all the ingredients are in the crock pot you can forget about it for two hours.

This dish is similar to beef pepper pot; however, cow foot is added which is the traditional way to prepare this Guyanese dish. More than one type of meat can be used when preparing this dish. The variety of meats and habanero added to this dish makes it even tastier. ***If you can stand the heat add extra habanero!***

Serve: Hot
Portion: 6-8 people
Cooking time: 1-2 hours, depending on your preference
Best with: Bread or by itself

Note: The amount of habanero pepper required may depend on the individual's preference.
½ habanero pepper = mild
1 habanero pepper = medium
2 habanero pepper = suicide

DEEP FRIED SALMON STEAKS

1 package salmon steaks (6-8 pieces)
Salt & black pepper to taste
2 tablespoons olive oil
1 teaspoon parsley flakes (fresh is best)
1 teaspoon oregano flakes (fresh is best)
1 teaspoon dried thyme (fresh is best)
½ habanero pepper, chopped

STEPS:

1. Salmon will need to be defrosted before cooking it, unless it is fresh.
2. Heat olive oil in a large sized frying pan, on high heat.
3. Season salmon steaks with spices and habanero. Thoroughly rub spices and habanero into the salmon steaks.
4. Turn heat down to medium, gently drop in salmon steaks and cook for one minute.
5. Cook evenly on both sides. *Please note that if salmon is cooked too long it will be overcooked.*

This is such a simple and tasty dish you would wonder why you never cooked salmon this way before. Delicious!

Serve: Hot
Portion: 4-6
Cooking time: 15 minutes
Best with: Rice or with pasta

Note: The amount of habanero pepper required may depend on the individual's preference.
½ habanero pepper = mild
1 habanero pepper = medium
2 habanero pepper = suicide

DEEP FRIED TALAPIA STEAKS

1 package tilapia steaks (10-15 pieces)
Salt & black pepper to taste
2 tablespoons olive oil
1 teaspoon parsley flakes (fresh is best)
1 teaspoon dried thyme (fresh is best)
1 teaspoon oregano flakes (fresh is best)
½ habanero pepper, chopped

STEPS:

1. Tilapia will need to be defrosted before it can be cooked, unless it is fresh.
2. Heat olive oil in a large sized frying pan, on high heat.
3. Season tilapia steaks with spice and habanero. Thoroughly rub spices and habanero into the tilapia steaks.
4. Turn heat down to medium, gently drop in tilapia steaks in frying pan and cook for one minute.
5. Cook evenly on both sides. *Please note that tilapia is a meaty fish and may require cooking it for at least two minutes on each side. Absolutely scrumptious!*

Serve: Hot
Portion: 8-10
Cooking time: 15 minutes
Best with: Rice or with pasta

Note: The amount of habanero pepper required may depend on the individual's preference.
½ habanero pepper = mild
1 habanero pepper = medium
2 habanero pepper = suicide

FRIED POTATOES & CORNED BEEF

3 medium potatoes (peel & thinly sliced)

1-12 oz. can corn beef

Salt & black pepper to taste

1 teaspoon parsley flakes

1 green onion, chopped

1 medium onion, chopped

1 medium tomato

2 tablespoons cooking oil (olive oil can be used)

½ habanero pepper, chopped

STEPS:

1. Peel and cut potatoes into thin slices.
2. Heat cooking oil in a medium sized frying pan, on high heat. Add the onion, green onion, habanero and cook until caramelized.
3. Add potatoes, salt, black pepper, parsley flakes and cook for approximately 15 minutes or until potatoes are done the way you like.
4. Add sliced tomato and cook for five minutes.
5. Add the corned beef and continue to cook on medium heat for 10 minutes.
6. Let cool for five minutes and serve.

Serve: Hot or Cold
Portion: 4-6 people
Cooking time: 20 minutes
Best with: Rice or Roti

Note: The amount of habanero pepper required may depend on the individual's preference.
½ habanero pepper = mild
1 habanero pepper = medium
2 habanero pepper = suicide

FRIED POTATOES & EGGS

5 medium potatoes

4 eggs

Salt & black pepper to taste

1 teaspoon parsley flakes (fresh is best)

1 teaspoon dried thyme (fresh is best)

1 green onion, chopped

1 medium onion, chopped

2 tablespoons cooking oil

1 medium tomato

½ habanero pepper, chopped

STEPS:

1. Peel and cut potatoes into thin slices.
2. In a medium sized bowl beat eggs with salt & black pepper and set aside.
3. Heat cooking oil in a medium sized frying pan; add the onion, green onion, habanero and cook until caramelized.
4. Add potatoes, salt, black pepper, thyme, parsley flakes and cook for approximately 15 minutes.
5. If potatoes are cooked to your satisfaction, add sliced tomato and cook for another five minutes.
6. Pour egg mixture evenly over potatoes and tomato; let it simmer on low heat for one minute.
7. Gently stir, ensure egg is evenly cooked.
8. Let cook for five minutes then serve.

This is a great way to serve eggs to those picky eaters. Guyanese eat this with roti in the mornings for breakfast, but it can be enjoyed anytime of the day!

Serve: Hot or Cold
Portion: 6-8 people
Cooking time: 20 minutes
Best with: Rice or Roti

Note: The amount of habanero pepper required may depend on the individual's preference.

½ habanero pepper = mild

1 habanero pepper = medium

2 habanero pepper = suicide

GROUND BEEF PIE

1 lb. ground beef
1 medium onion, chopped
1 package taco seasoning
1-4 oz. can chop green chilies
1 cup shredded Monterey Jack cheese (split into ¾ cup and ¼ cup)
3 eggs
1-¼ cup milk
¾ cup pancake mix
Non-stick cooking spray
1 habanero pepper, chopped

STEPS:

1. Preheat oven to 350°F.
2. Brown the ground beef, onion and habanero in a medium sized pot.
3. If necessary drain fat off. Mix in taco seasoning *(no need to add water, it may seem dry, but liquid will be added later)*
4. Spray a pie plate with non-stick cooking spray and line with meat and onion.
5. Spread the green chilies over top of the meat.
6. Layer ¾ cup of the shredded cheese over the green chilies.
7. Place eggs, milk and pancake mix in a blender and mix on high for 30 seconds.
8. Pour evenly over top of the cheese.
9. Bake in oven for approximately 20 minutes.
10. Sprinkle the remaining ¼ cup cheese over the top
11. Bake for additional five minutes until top is golden brown. Ready to eat!

Best served hot
Serves: 4-6people
Cooking time: 25 minutes
Best with: main course of by itself

Note: The amount of habanero pepper required may depend on the individual's preference.
½ habanero pepper = mild
1 habanero pepper = medium
2 habanero pepper = suicide

SCALLOPED POTATOES

4 medium potatoes (thinly sliced)
1 can condense cream of mushroom soup
¼ cup milk
1 teaspoon Italian seasoning
2 cloves garlic, crushed
¼ cup grated parmesan cheese
1 medium onion, chopped
1 green onion, chopped
½ cup shredded mozzarella cheese
Salt & pepper to taste
½ habanero pepper, chopped

STEPS:
1. In greased medium sized casserole dish, arrange half of potatoes and half onion.
2. Sprinkle with half of the mozzarella cheese & half parmesan cheese.
3. In small bowl combine condensed soup, milk, Italian seasoning, habanero, garlic and salt/pepper and spoon over the potato mixture.
4. Cover and bake at 350°F for approximately 20 minutes.
5. Uncover and cook for an additional 10 minutes or until potatoes are golden brown.

Serve: Hot or Cold
Portion: 4-6
Cooking time: 30 minutes
Best with: Meatloaf or Roast

Note: The amount of habanero pepper required may depend on the individual's preference.
½ habanero pepper = mild
1 habanero pepper = medium
2 habanero pepper = suicide

LASAGNA

1 lb. lasagna noodles 1 tablespoon olive oil

2 lbs. ground beef (substitute with ground turkey) 1 medium onion, chopped

1 package frozen spinach 2 celery stalks, chopped

4 cloves garlic, chopped Salt & black pepper to taste

1 teaspoon dried oregano, basil & thyme 2-8oz cans tomato sauce

2 teaspoons nutmeg 2 eggs

2-8oz. cans tomatoes (do not drain off water) 2 cups mozzarella cheese

1 habanero pepper, chopped 1 cup freshly grated parmesan cheese

2 cups cottage cheese 2 cups ricotta cheese

STEPS:

1. In a large pot of salted boiling water add olive oil and cook lasagna noodles for approximately 10 minutes or until tender.
2. Drain in colander and run cold water through noodles.
3. Arrange in single layer on damp tea towel and set aside.
4. Set oven to 375°F.
5. Cook ground meat on medium heat for approximately 10 minutes. *Drain off excess fat if necessary.*

6. Add the onion, garlic, carrots, celery, spinach, oregano, basil, thyme, salt, black pepper, habanero, and half of the nutmeg.

7. Add tomatoes and tomato sauce.

8. Reduce heat to low and let it simmer for 20 minutes.

9. In medium sized bowl beat eggs, salt and pepper and remaining nutmeg. Add in cottage cheese, ricotta cheese and mozzarella.

10. Spread one cup of the meat filling as a base in medium sized baking dish. Top with 1/3 of the noodles in single layer. Spread meat sauce on top of the noodles then spread with cheese filling. Repeat this process at least twice or as many times as you desire.

11. The top layer should be cheese.

12. Cover loosely with foil; bake at 375ºF for approximately 30 minutes.

13. Uncover and bake for another 10 minutes or until sizzling or cooked all the way through.

Serve: Hot or Cold
Portion: 6-8 people
Cooking time: 60 minutes
Best with: Garlic Bread

Note: The amount of habanero pepper required may depend on the individual's preference.
½ habanero pepper = mild
1 habanero pepper = medium
2 habanero pepper = suicide

MEATLOAF

2 lbs. ground beef (any ground meat can be substituted)
1 onion soup mix
1 medium onion, chopped
1 green onion, chopped
1 cup bread crumb
½ cup ketchup
2 eggs
Salt & pepper to taste
1 habanero pepper, chopped

STEPS:
1. Set oven to 350°F.
2. Mix all ingredients together.
3. Put mixed ingredients into a loft pan and bake for approximately 30 minutes.

Not only is this dish delicious but it is also quick and easy to prepare. It is ideal for those busy week nights. The entire family can have a sit down meal in no time!

Best served hot
Portion: 6-8 people
Cooking time: 30 minutes
Best with: Potatoes and vegetables

Note: The amount of habanero pepper required may depend on the individual's preference.
½ habanero pepper = mild
1 habanero pepper = medium
2 habanero pepper = suicide

SLINKY POTATOES

4 medium potatoes
Salt & black pepper to taste
1 tablespoon melted butter
2 green onions, chopped
4 tablespoons grated cheddar cheese
1 tablespoon grated parmesan cheese
1 teaspoon dried habanero pepper

STEPS:

1. Scrub potatoes and cut them crosswise into thin slices, but not all the way through. *The potatoes should barely be holding together on the bottom and open along the top.*

2. Carefully place the potatoes in a baking dish and fan the slices out slightly.

3. Sprinkle the potatoes with salt, black pepper, habanero, chives and drizzle with butter.

4. Set oven to 375°F and bake for approximately 25 minutes. *Occasionally, base the potato with the butter on the bottom of the pan.*

5. Remove potatoes from the oven, sprinkle with cheese and bake for another 10 minutes until lightly browned and soft inside. Ready to eat!

Serve: Hot
Portion: 4
Cooking time: 40 minutes
Best with: Spicy meatloaf, roast or spicy chicken

Note: The amount of habanero pepper required may depend on the individual's preference.
½ habanero pepper = mild
1 habanero pepper = medium
2 habanero pepper = suicide

Chicken Curry

DELECTABLE DINNERS

BEEF CURRY

1 lb. stewing beef, cubed
Salt & black pepper to taste
2 green onions, chopped
1 medium onion, chopped
2 tablespoons cooking oil
2 tablespoons white vinegar
2 tablespoons curry powder
2 cloves garlic, crushed
2-3 medium potatoes
Water
1 habanero pepper, chopped

STEPS:

1. Wash meat with vinegar and water.
2. Drain into a colander.
3. In a small bowl add the onion, green onion, habanero, garlic; mix together with curry powder and half cup water.
4. Heat cooking oil in a deep, medium sized pot (or wok), but wait until oil is very hot before adding curry powder mixture. Cover pot and let mixture brown for approximately five minutes.

5. Peel and quarter potatoes.
6. When curry mixture is golden brown *not burnt* add beef and potatoes. Cook on medium heat for 15 minutes, stirring occasionally.
7. Add two cups of boiling water into pot and taste for salt, if more salt is needed then add; cook on medium heat for another 30 minutes or until beef is sufficiently cooked.
8. If there is more gravy then you desire let it boil until excess water is removed.

Serve: Hot or Cold
Portion: 4-6 people
Cooking time: 45 minutes
Best with: Plain rice or Any Roti

Note: The amount of habanero pepper required may depend on the individual's preference.
½ habanero pepper = mild
1 habanero pepper = medium
2 habanero pepper = suicide

BLACK EYE PEAS/COOK-UP

1 cup black eye peas

1 cup rice

Salt & black pepper to taste

1-8 oz. can kidney beans

1 habanero pepper, chopped

1 lb. beef (other meat may be substituted to suite your preference)

½ cup coconut cream (coconut milk can be substituted)

1 medium onion, chopped

1 green onion, chopped

1 teaspoon parsley (fresh is best)

1 teaspoon dried thyme (fresh is best)

2 tablespoons cooking oil

STEPS:

1. In a medium bowl, add two cups of water and black eye peas and let it soak for approximately one hour before cooking. *This is best if black eye peas are soaked overnight.*
2. Next day, use a deep medium sized pot; add three cups of water and black eye peas and cook for approximately 20 minutes.
3. In the same bowl wash rice and add into the pot, stir occasionally.
4. Heat cooking oil in a medium sized frying pan; add the onion and green onion and cook for three minutes until caramelized.
5. Add beef in the frying pan and cook for 10 minutes.
6. Add contents from frying pan into the pot with black eye peas and rice.
7. Add coconut cream *(coconut milk can also be used).*
8. Add habanero, parsley flakes, thyme and salt & black pepper.
9. Cook on medium heat for at least 30 minutes or until rice is boiled to you satisfaction, *(stir often so rice/black eye peas does not stick to the pot or burn).*
10. Let cool for five minutes and you have a pot of delicious cook-up ready to be served to family and friends!

Serve: Hot or Cold

Portion: 5-8

Cooking time: 60 minutes

Best with: Chutney

CHUTNEY

1 medium tomato
2 tablespoons lemon juice or vinegar
1 habanero
1 medium onion
1 teaspoon salt
2 cloves garlic

STEP: Add all ingredients in a blender and blend until the consistency is smooth. Remove in a bowl and serve with meal.

Note: The amount of habanero pepper required may depend on the individual's preference.

½ habanero pepper = mild

1 habanero pepper = medium

2 habanero pepper = suicide

BOIL & FRY (PROVISION)

2 ripe plantains
4 medium eddoes
2 small tania (sweet potatoes/yams)
2 medium sized cassava or ½ package frozen
1 cup all-purpose flour
1 teaspoon baking powder
1 medium onion, chopped
1 lb. salted cod fish
2 tablespoons cooking oil
1 habanero pepper, chopped
Codfish will be salted do not add salt

STEPS:
1. Peel and quarter the eddoes, plantains, and tanias (sweet potatoes/yams).
2. Mix flour and baking powder together and kneed with half a cup of water. Dough should hae same consistency as pizza dough.
3. Use your hands to roll dough into ball or long dumplings and set aside.
4. Add three cups of water to a large sized pot and boil on medium heat.
5. Add cassava & eddoes (*provisions)* to boiling water and cook for 10 minutes.
6. Add sweet potatoes & plantains (*provisions*) and cook for another 10 minutes.
7. Add dumplings to pot and cook for five minutes or until dumplings are evenly cooked.
8. Drain contents of pot into colander and set aside.
9. In a small pot add one cup water and salted cod fish.
10. Let this boil for five minutes (*boiling the salted cod fish will remove some of the salt*). Drain in colander.
11. Let cool, then cut into bite size pieces.
12. Add cooking oil to the large sized pot, on medium heat; add the onion, habanero, salt fish and cook for 10 minutes or until the salt fish is golden brown. Turn heat down to low.
13. Add reserved cassavas, plantains, eddoes and sweet potatoes (*provisions*) and dumplings. This will be tricky to stir, cautiously flip the pot so provisions are mixed together with salt fish.

14. Remove from heat to cool and serve!

This unique dish consists of root vegetables (referred to as provisions), which are grown in Guyana. Guyanese enjoy this meal as breakfast on Saturdays or Sundays but again it can be eaten anytime!

Serve: Hot or Cold
Portion: 6-8 people
Cooking time: 45 minutes
Best with: Gilbaka curry (*recipe on page 54*)

DEPENDING ON YOUR PREFERENCE ANY OF THE ABOVE VEGETABLE CAN BE SUBSTITUTED.

Note: The amount of habanero pepper required may depend on the individual's preference.
½ habanero pepper = mild
1 habanero pepper = medium
2 habanero pepper = suicide

BORA (LONG BEAN) & CHICKEN CURRY

1 chicken, cut into bite sized pieces (legs or breast can be substituted)
1 handful bora (long beans)
Salt & black pepper to taste
2 green onions, chopped
1 medium onion, chopped
2 tablespoons cooking oil
2 tablespoons white vinegar
2 tablespoons curry powder
2 cloves garlic (crushed)
2-3 medium potatoes
Water
1 habanero pepper, chopped

STEPS:
1. Wash chicken with vinegar and water.
2. Drain into colander and set aside.
3. Wash and cut ends off bora (*long beans*), then cut into small pieces (*depending on your preference*).
4. In a small bowl add the onion, green onion, habanero, garlic and mix together with curry powder and half cup water.

5. Heat the cooking oil in a medium sized pot (or wok), on high heat. Wait until oil is very hot before adding curry powder mixture and cook for three minutes. Turn heat down to medium.

6. Peel and quarter potatoes and set aside.

7. Add chicken, bora (*long beans*) and potatoes and continue to cook on medium heat for approximately 15 minutes, stirring occasionally.

8. Add one cup water, taste for salt, if more needed then add.

9. Continue to cook on medium heat for another 15 minutes.

10. If there is more gravy then you desire, boil curry until water is gone to your likening. If you need more gravy just add some water.

11. Let cool five minutes and enjoy this unique Guyanese vegetable!

Serve: Hot or Cold
Portion: 4-6 people
Cooking time: 30 minutes, plus preparation time
Best with: Plain rice or Any Roti

Note: The amount of habanero pepper required may depend on the individual's preference.
½ habanero pepper = mild
1 habanero pepper = medium
2 habanero pepper = suicide

CHANNA CURRY

2-8 oz. cans chick peas (garbanzo beans)
Salt & black pepper to taste
2 green onion, chopped
1 medium onion, chopped
3 medium potatoes
2 carrots, diced (optional)
2 tablespoons cooking oil
2 tablespoons curry powder
2 cloves garlic, crushed
1 habanero pepper, chopped

STEPS:

1. In a small bowl, add the onion, green onion, habanero, garlic and curry powder with half cup of water.
2. Peel and dice potatoes and carrots and set aside.
3. Heat cooking oil in a medium sized pot, on high heat. Wait until oil is very hot before adding in the curry powder mixture. Cook for three minutes on medium heat.
4. Add potatoes, carrots and half cup water and continue to cook on medium heat for 10 minutes.
5. Add the chick peas and cook for another 10 minutes or until vegetables are cooked as desire.
6. Let cool for five minutes and serve!

Serve: Hot or Cold
Portion: 4-6 people
Cooking time: 25 minutes
Best with: Plain rice or Any Roti

Note: The amount of habanero pepper required may depend on the individual's preference.
½ habanero pepper = mild
1 habanero pepper = medium
2 habanero pepper = suicide

CHICKEN CURRY

1 chicken, cut into bite sized pieces (legs, breasts can be substituted)
Sat & black pepper to taste
2 green onions, chopped
1 medium onion, chopped
2 tablespoons cooking oil
2 tablespoons white vinegar
2 tablespoons curry powder
2 cloves garlic, crushed
2-3 medium potatoes
Water
1 habanero pepper, chopped

STEPS:

1. Wash chicken with vinegar and water and drain into colander.
2. In a small bowl add the onion, green onion, habanero, and garlic mix together with curry powder and half cup water.
3. Heat cooking oil in a medium sized pot, on high heat. Add curry powder mixture and cook for three minutes.
4. Peel and quarter potatoes and set aside.
5. Add chicken and potatoes and cook on medium heat for 15 minutes, stirring occasionally.
6. Add one cup of water and taste for salt, if more needed then add. Cook on medium heat for approximately 30 minutes or until chicken is cooked the way you like.
7. If there is more gravy than you desire, then let curry boil until water dries down to your likening. If you need more gravy just add water.
8. Let cool and enjoy this delicious meal!

Serve: Hot or Cold
Portion: 4-6 people
Cooking time: 45 minutes, plus preparation time
Best with: Plain rice or Any Roti

Note: The amount of habanero pepper required may depend on the individual's preference.

½ habanero pepper = mild

1 habanero pepper = medium

2 habanero pepper = suicide

CHICKEN FRIED RICE

1 lb. boneless chicken breast (cubed)

2 cups basmati rice (any rice will do)

Salt & pepper to taste

2 green onions, chopped

1 medium onion, chopped

2 tablespoons cooking oil

2 cloves garlic, crushed

¼ cup frozen mixed vegetables (fresh vegetables may be substituted)

5 tablespoons mushroom sauce (Soya sauce maybe be substituted)

1 habanero pepper, chopped

STEPS:

1. Wash chicken, drain into colander and set aside.
2. In a medium sized, deep pot, boil rice for 10 minutes. Rice must be loose not too soft or sticky. Drain rice in colander, add mixed vegetables and set aside.
3. Heat cooking oil in a medium sized pot, on high heat; add the onion, green onion, habanero, garlic and cook until caramelized.
4. Add chicken and cook on medium heat for 15 minutes or until all liquid is evaporated, stirring occasionally.
5. Add rice and vegetables; stir in mushroom sauce (Soya sauce) and cook on low heat for another 10 minutes. Ready to serve!

Serve: Hot or Cold
Portion: 6-8 people
Cooking time: 35 minutes, plus preparation time
Best with: Chutney

CHUTNEY

1 medium tomato

½ habanero

1 teaspoon salt

½ medium onion

3 cloves garlic

STEP: Add all ingredients in a blender and blend until consistency is smooth. Remove in a bowl and serve with dish.

Note: The amount of habanero pepper required may depend on the individual's preference.
½ **habanero pepper = mild**
1 **habanero pepper = medium**
2 **habanero pepper = suicide**

DUCK CURRY

1 medium size duck (cut into pieces)
Salt & black pepper to taste
2 green onions, chopped
1 medium onion, chopped
2 tablespoons cooking oil
2 tablespoons white vinegar
2 tablespoons curry powder
2 cloves garlic, crushed
2-3 medium potatoes
Water
1 habanero pepper, chopped

STEPS:

1. Wash meat with vinegar and water, drain into colander and set aside.
2. Mix the onion, green onion, habanero, and garlic together with curry powder and half cup water.
3. Heat cooking oil in a medium sized pot, on high heat; add curry mixture and cook for approximately three minutes, until brown.
4. Peel and quarter potatoes.
5. Add duck meat and potatoes and cook on medium heat for 15 minutes, stirring occasionally.
6. Add two cup water and taste for salt, if more needed then add. Cook on low heat for approximately one hour or until duck is cooked the way you like. More water may be needed to ensure that the duck meat is tender.

Serve: Hot or Cold
Portion: 4-6 people
Cooking time: 90 minutes
Best with: Plain rice or Any Roti

Note: The amount of habanero pepper required may depend on the individual's preference.
½ habanero pepper = mild
🌶 1 habanero pepper = medium
🌶🌶2 habanero pepper = suicide

EDDOES & SHRIMP CURRY

1 package jumbo tiger shrimp (fresh tiger shrimp can be used)
5-7 medium eddoes
Salt to taste
2 green onions, chopped
1 medium onion, chopped
2 tablespoons cooking oil
2 tablespoons white vinegar
2 tablespoons curry powder
2 cloves garlic, crushed
2-3 medium potatoes
Water
1 habanero pepper, chopped

STEPS:

1. Cut off the head and tail of the shrimp.
2. Wash shrimp with vinegar and water.
3. Drain into colander and set aside.
4. Mix the onion, green onion, habanero, and garlic together with curry powder and half cup water.
5. Heat cooking oil in a medium sized pot, on high heat; add curry powder mixture and cook for three minutes.
6. Peel and quarter eddoes.
7. Add eddoes and shrimp and cook on medium heat for five minutes, stirring occasionally.
8. Add one cup water and taste for salt, if more needed then add. Cook on medium heat for approximately 20 minutes or until eddoes are cooked the way you like.
9. If there is more gravy than you desire, then let curry boil until water dries down to your likening. If more gravy is needed just add water.
10. Let cool for five minutes and enjoy this delicious meal!

Serve: Hot or Cold
Portion: 4-6 people
Cooking time: 30 minutes
Best with: Plain rice or Any Roti

Note: The amount of habanero pepper required may depend on the individual's preference.

½ habanero pepper = mild

1 habanero pepper = medium

2 habanero pepper = suicide

EGGPLANT/ POTATOES & CHICKEN

1 medium size eggplant

4 medium potatoes

1 boneless chicken breast, cubed (shrimp or beef can be substituted)

Salt & black pepper to taste

2 tablespoons cooking oil

1 green onion, chopped

1 tablespoons white vinegar

1 medium onion, chopped

1 medium tomato, chopped

1 chopped habanero pepper

STEPS:

1. Peel and slice eggplant into small pieces and set aside.
2. Wash meat with vinegar and water.
3. Drain meat in colander and set aside.
4. Peel potatoes and cut into thin slices.
5. Heat cooking oil in a medium sized frying pan on high heat. Add the onion, green onion and habanero and cook for one minute on medium heat.
6. Add chicken and cook for another 10 minutes.
7. Add eggplant, potatoes, salt & black pepper and continue to cook on medium heat for 10 minutes, stirring occasionally.
8. Add tomatoes and cook on low heat for another 15 minutes or until eggplant and potatoes are cooked the way you like.
9. Let cool for five minutes before you serve.

Serve: Hot or Cold

Portion: 4-6 people

Cooking time: 40 minutes

Best with: Plain rice or Roti

Note: The amount of habanero pepper required may depend on the individual's preference.

½ habanero pepper = mild

1 habanero pepper = medium

2 habanero pepper = suicide

EGGPLANT/ EDDOES & SHRIMP CURRY

1 package jumbo tiger shrimp (fresh shrimp can be substituted)
1 large egg plant
4-5 medium eddoes
Salt to taste
2 green onions, chopped
1 medium onion, chopped
2 tablespoons cooking oil
2 tablespoons white vinegar
2 tablespoons curry powder
2 cloves garlic, crushed
2-3 medium potatoes
Water
1 habanero pepper, chopped

STEPS:
1. Remove heads and tails from shrimp.
2. Wash shrimp with vinegar and water.
3. Drain into colander and set aside.
4. Peel and thinly slice eggplant and set aside.
5. In a small bowl add the onion, green onion, habanero, and garlic together with curry powder and half cup water.
6. Heat cooking oil in a medium sized pot, on high heat; add curry powder mixture and cook for approximately three minutes.
7. Peel and quarter eddoes.
8. Add eggplant, eddoes and shrimp. Cook on medium heat for five minutes, stirring occasionally.
9. Add one cup water and taste for salt, if more needed then add. Cook on low heat for another 20 minutes or until eddoes are cooked the way you like.
10. If there is more gravy than you desire, then let curry boil until water dries down to your likening. If more gravy is needed just add water and continue to boil.
11. Let cool for five minutes before you can enjoy this delicious meal!

Serve: Hot or Cold
Portion: 4-6 people

Cooking time: 30 minutes
Best with: Plain rice or Any Roti

Note: The amount of habanero pepper required may depend on the individual's preference.
½ habanero pepper = mild
1 habanero pepper = medium
2 habanero pepper = suicide

FRIED BORA (LONG BEANS) & CHICKEN

1 handful of bora (long beans)
4 medium potatoes
1 boneless chicken breast, cubed (shrimp or beef can be substituted)
Salt & black pepper to taste
2 tablespoons cooking oil
1 green onion, chopped
2 tablespoons white vinegar
1 medium onion, chopped
1 medium tomato
1 habanero pepper, chopped

STEPS:

1. Cut tops and bottoms off bora (long beans), then cut into small pieces.
2. Wash meat with vinegar and water.
3. Drain in colander and set aside.
4. Peel potatoes and cut into thin slices and set aside.
5. Heat cooking oil in a medium sized pot, on high heat; add the onion, green onion and habanero until caramelized.
6. Add chicken and cook on medium heat for 10 minutes.

7. Add bora (*long beans*), potatoes, salt and black pepper and cook for an additional 15 minutes, stirring occasionally.
8. Add sliced tomato and cook for another 10 minutes or until bora (*long beans*) and potatoes are cooked as you desire.
9. Let cool for ten minutes before serving.

Serve: Hot or Cold
Portion: 4-6 people
Cooking time: 35-40 minutes
Best with: Plain rice or Roti

Note: The amount of habanero pepper required may depend on the individual's preference.
½ habanero pepper = mild
1 habanero pepper = medium
2 habanero pepper = suicide

FRIED GREEN BEANS & CHICKEN

2 hand full green beans
2 boneless chicken breasts, cubed (shrimp or beef may be substituted)
2 tablespoons vinegar
Salt & black pepper to taste
1 medium onion, chopped
1 green onion, chopped
1 medium tomato
2 teaspoons tomato paste
4 medium potatoes (peeled & thinly sliced)
2 tablespoons cooking oil
1 habanero pepper, chopped

STEPS:

1. Cut top and bottom off green beans; then cut into 4 pieces and set aside.
2. Wash chicken with vinegar and water.
3. Drain chicken in colander and set aside.
4. Peel potatoes and cut into thin slices.
5. Heat cooking oil in a medium sized pot, on high heat. Add the onion, green onion, habanero and cook for one minute or until caramelized.
6. Add green beans, potatoes, salt, tomato paste & black pepper and cook for 20 minutes on medium heat, stirring occasional.
7. Add sliced tomato and cook 10 minutes until green beans and potatoes are cooked to your liking.
8. Let cool for five minutes before serving.

Serve: Hot or Cold
Portion: 4-6 people
Cooking time: 35 minutes
Best with: Plain rice or Any Roti

Note: The amount of habanero pepper required may depend on the individual's preference.
½ habanero pepper = mild
1 habanero pepper = medium
2 habanero pepper = suicide

FRIED OKRA & SHRIMP

2 small baskets of okra (25-30 okras)

1 lb. package shrimp (chicken or beef can be substituted)

2 tablespoons white vinegar

Salt & black pepper to taste

2 tablespoons cooking oil

1 green onion, chopped

1 medium onion, chopped

1 medium tomato

1 habanero pepper, chopped

Okra with beef

STEPS:

1. Cut top and bottom off okra; then cut into small pieces or as you desire.

2. Remove heads and tails from shrimp.

3. Wash with vinegar and water, drain in colander and set aside.

4. Heat cooking oil in a medium sized frying pan, on high heat. Add the onion, green onion and habanero and let simmer for one minute or until caramelized.

5. Add shrimp and cook for five minutes.

6. Add okra, salt and black pepper and cook for 10 minutes on medium to low heat, stirring occasionally.
7. Add sliced tomato and cook on low heat for an additional 15 minutes, or until okras are cooked to you preference.
8. Let cool and serve.

Serve: Hot or Cold
Portion: 4-6 people
Cooking time: 30 minutes
Best with: Plain rice or Roti

Note: The amount of habanero pepper required may depend on the individual's preference.
½ habanero pepper = mild
1 habanero pepper = medium
2 habanero pepper = suicide

GILBAKA (FISH) CURRY

1 package gilbaka, cut into bite size pieces (or fresh gilbaka)
Salt to taste
2 green onions, chopped
1 medium onion, chopped
2 tablespoons cooking oil
2 tablespoons white vinegar
2 tablespoons curry powder
2 cloves garlic, crushed
6 whole okras (tops & bottoms cut off)
Water
1 habanero pepper, chopped

STEPS:

This fish is one of the uniqueness Guyana has to offer. Gilbaka is very tasty and does not have any fine bones that most fish has, so it very safe to eat. There is no fear about getting a bone stuck in your throat. The meat is absolutely delicious and once you cook it this way you will always want more!

1. Wash gilbaka (fish) with vinegar and water.
2. Drain into colander and set aside.
3. Mix the onion, green onion, habanero, and garlic together with curry powder and half cup water.
4. Heat cooking oil into a medium sized pot, on high heat. Add curry mixture and cook for approximately five minutes.
5. Add the fish and cook on medium heat for 10 minutes, gently stirring.
6. Add one cup of water into pot and taste for salt, if more needed then add. Cook on medium heat for approximately 20 minutes.
7. Add okras and cook another 10 minutes.
8. If there is more gravy then you desire let curry boil until water dries down to your likening. If you need more gravy, just add water and boil.
9. *Let cool, then enjoy this very unique tasting Guyanese fish!*

Serve: Hot or Cold
Portion: 4-6 people
Cooking time: 45 minutes

Best with: Plain rice or Any Roti

Note: The amount of habanero pepper required may depend on the individual's preference.
½ habanero pepper = mild
  1 habanero pepper = medium
2 habanero pepper = suicide

GOAT CURRY

1 lb. goat meat, cut into bite size pieces
Salt to taste
2 green onions, chopped
1 medium onion, chopped
2 tablespoons cooking oil
2 tablespoons white vinegar
2 tablespoons curry powder
2 cloves garlic, crushed
2-3 medium potatoes
Water
1 habanero pepper, chopped

STEPS:

1. Wash meat with vinegar and water.
2. Drain in colander and set aside.
3. In a small bowl add the onion, green onion, habanero, garlic and mix together with curry powder and half cup water.
4. Heat cooking oil in a medium sized pot, on high heat. Add curry mixture and cook for approximately three minutes.
5. Peel and quarter potatoes.
6. Add the goat meat and potatoes. Cook on medium heat for 15 minutes, stirring occasionally.
7. Add two cups of water and taste for salt, if more needed then add.
8. Continue to cook on medium heat for approximately 40 minutes or until meat is tender.
9. If there is more gravy than you desire, then let curry boil until water dries down to your likening. If more gravy is required, just add water and continue to boil.
10. Let cool before you serve this unique meat!

   Even if goat is not your meat of choice, cooking it curried (Guyanese style) will allow you to enjoy this dish without having any second thoughts!

Serve: Hot or Cold
Portion: 4-6 people
Cooking time: 60 minutes
Best with: Plain rice or Any Roti

Note: The amount of habanero pepper required may depend on the individual's preference.

½ habanero pepper = mild

1 habanero pepper = medium

2 habanero pepper = suicide

HASSA (FISH) CURRY

6 medium sized hassas
Salt to taste
2 green onion, chopped
1 medium onion, chopped
2 tablespoons cooking oil
2 tablespoons white vinegar
2 tablespoons curry powder
2 cloves garlic, crushed
1-8oz. can coconut milk (fresh coconut milk or coconut cream can be used)
Water
1 habanero pepper, chopped

STEPS:

Hassas are yet another unique feature of Guyana. This fish is ugly and have outer bones but once they are cooked the bones easily comes off. There are some small bones but for the most part it is meaty.

Cleaning the Hassas may be a little challenging if you are not familiar with it, but it is worth it once you taste this succulent fish. So if you are adventurous and want to try something new, I suggest trying Hassa.

1. Cut and clean inside of hassas (*use a cooking shear to help cut the fins and tails off the hassas*).
2. Wash hassas with vinegar and water.
3. Drain into colander and set aside.
4. In a small bowl, add the onion, green onion, garlic, habanero, garlic and mix together with curry powder and half cup water.
5. Heat cooking oil in a medium sized pot, on high heat. Add curry mixture and cook for five minutes.
6. Add hassas and cook on medium heat for 10 minutes, gently stirring.
7. Add one cup of water and coconut milk (*coconut cream can be used*) and taste for salt, if more needed then add. Cook on low heat for approximately 20 minutes.
8. If there is more gravy then you desire let curry boil until water dries to your likening. If more gravy is needed, just add water and continue to boil.
9. Let cool for five minutes then serve.

This is my favorite fish curry dish! Once the fish is cooked the top bones will fall off, allowing you to eat the mouthwatering, sweet meat of the hassa.

Serve: Hot or Cold
Portion: 4-6 people
Cooking time: 35 minutes
Best with: Plain rice or Any Roti

Note: The amount of habanero pepper required may depend on the individual's preference.
½ habanero pepper = mild
1 habanero pepper = medium
2 habanero pepper = suicide

KALOUNGI (KARILA CURRY)

1 pound stewing beef, cubed (ground beef can be substituted)
4-5 medium karila
Salt to taste
2 green onions, chopped
1 medium onion, chopped
2 tablespoons cooking oil
2 tablespoons white vinegar
2 tablespoons curry powder
2 cloves garlic, crushed
¼ frozen coconut cream (coconut milk is best)
Water
1 habanero pepper, crushed

STEPS:

1. Wash beef/ground beef with vinegar and water.
2. Drain into colander and set aside.
3. Use a potato peeler to scrape off the bumpy top skin of karila (a knife can be used).
4. In a small bowl, add the onion, green onion, habanero, garlic and mix with curry powder and half cup water.
5. In a medium sized frying pan fry beef or ground beef on medium heat, until brown. Add half of the curry power mixture and cook for 10 minutes, then set aside.
6. Slit open one side of the karilas and stuff with beef/ground beef mixture.
7. Heat cooking oil in a medium sized pot, on high heat. Add remaining curry powder mixture and cook for three minutes.
8. Add stuffed karila, coconut cream and cook on medium heat for 15 minutes, stirring occasionally.
9. Add one cup of water and taste for salt, if more needed then add. Cook on medium heat for approximately 20 minutes.
10. If there is more gravy then you desire let curry boil until water dries down to your likening.

Serve: Hot or Cold
Portion: 4-6 people

Cooking time: 45 minutes
Best with: Plain rice or Any Roti

Note: The amount of habanero pepper required may depend on the individual's preference.

½ habanero pepper = mild

1 habanero pepper = medium

2 habanero pepper = suicide

LIVER CURRY (CHICKEN)

1 lb. liver (either chicken or beef liver can be used)
Salt to taste
2 green onions, chopped
1 medium onion, chopped
2 tablespoons cooking oil
2 tablespoons white vinegar
2 tablespoons curry powder
2 cloves garlic, crushed
1 habanero pepper, chopped

STEPS:

1. Wash liver with vinegar and water.
2. Drain into colander and set aside.
2. In a small bowl add the onion, green onion, habanero, and garlic together with curry powder and a half cup of water.
3. Heat cooking oil in a small pot, on high heat. Add the curry mixture and cook for about three minutes.
4. Add liver and cook on medium heat for 15 minutes, stirring occasionally. Ready to serve!

My children do not like liver, but when I curry it they absolutely love it!

Serve: Hot or Cold
Portion: 4-6 people
Cooking time: 20 minutes
Best with: Plain rice or Any Roti

Note: The amount of habanero pepper required may depend on the individual's preference.
½ habanero pepper = mild
1 habanero pepper = medium
2 habanero pepper = suicide

MUTTON (LAMB) CURRY

1 lb. mutton (lamb)
Salt to taste
2 green onions, chopped
1 medium onion, chopped
2 tablespoons cooking oil
2 tablespoons white vinegar
2 tablespoons curry powder
2 cloves garlic, crushed
2-3 medium potatoes
Water
1 habanero pepper, chopped

STEPS:

1. Cut meat into bite size pieces if not already done.
2. Wash meat with vinegar and water.
3. Drain into colander and set aside.
4. In a small bowl add the onion, green onion, habanero, and garlic together with curry powder and half cup of water.
5. Heat cooking oil in a medium sized pot, on medium heat. Add the curry mixture and cook for about five minutes.
6. Peel and quarter potatoes.
7. Add meat and potatoes and cook on medium heat for 15 minutes, stirring occasionally.
8. Add water and taste for salt, if more needed then add. Continue to cook on medium heat for approximately 40 minutes or until the meat is tender.
9. If there is more gravy then you desire let curry boil until water dries down to your likening.

This is an excellent way to prepare lamb because the curry brings out the flavor in the meat enabling you to enjoy all the delicious flavors!

Serve: Hot or Cold
Portion: 4-6 people
Cooking time: 50-60 minutes
Best with: Plain rice or Any Roti

Note: The amount of habanero pepper required may depend on the individual's preference.

½ habanero pepper = mild

1 habanero pepper = medium

2 habanero pepper = suicide

SAME & SHRIMP CURRY

1 package jumbo tiger shrimp (or fresh shrimp)

2 lbs. same

Salt to taste

2 green onions, chopped

1 medium onion, chopped

2 tablespoons cooking oil

2 tablespoons white vinegar

2 tablespoons curry powder

2 cloves garlic, crushed

¼ frozen coconut cream (or coconut milk)

2-3 medium potatoes

Water

1 habanero pepper, chopped

STEPS:

1. Defrost shrimp and remove heads and tails. *If you are using fresh shrimp follow the same instructions.*

2. Wash shrimp with vinegar and water.

3. Drain into colander and set aside.

4. Wash and cut ends off the same, and then cut into two.

5. In a small bowl add the onion, green onion, habanero, and garlic together with curry powder in half cup water.

6. Heat cooking oil in a medium sized pot, on high heat. Add the curry mixture and cook for five minutes.

7. Peel and quarter potatoes.

8. Add the shrimp, same, coconut cream and potatoes; cook on medium heat for 15 minutes, stirring occasionally.

9. Add one cup of water into pot and taste for salt, if more needed then add. Cook on medium heat for approximately 20 minutes.

10. If there is more gravy then you desire let curry boil until water dries down to your likening.

The same is a native vegetable from Guyana. In Guyana it is cooked with fresh shrimp and fresh coconut milk. There is a unique flavor to this vegetable that you will absolutely love!

Serve: Hot or Cold
Portion: 4-6 people
Cooking time: 40 minutes
Best with: Plain rice or Any Roti

Note: The amount of habanero pepper required may depend on the individual's preference.
½ habanero pepper = mild
1 habanero pepper = medium
2 habanero pepper = suicide

SHRIMP FRIED RICE

3 lbs. tiger shrimp 2 cups basmati rice (any rice will do)
2 hand full of frozen peas & carrots Salt & black pepper to taste
1 teaspoon parsley flakes (fresh is best) 4 tablespoons mushroom sauce
2 tablespoons dark Soya sauce 1 medium onion, chopped
2 green onions, chopped 2 cloves garlic, crushed
2 tablespoons cooking oil 1 habanero pepper, chopped
1 teaspoon dried thyme (fresh is best)

STEPS:

1. Cut heads and tails and peel shrimp.
2. Wash with vinegar and water.
3. Drain into colander and set aside.
4. Boil rice for 15 minutes until the grain is gone (not soft or sticky).
5. Drain into colander; add mixed vegetables and set aside.
6. Heat cooking oil in a medium sized pot, on high heat. Add the onion, green onion, habanero and garlic and cook until caramelized.
7. Add the shrimp and cook on medium heat 10 minutes, stirring occasionally.

8. Add the rice, vegetables, mushroom sauce and soya sauce; then cook for an additional 10 minutes.
9. Let cool for five minutes then enjoy!

Serve: Hot or Cold
Portion: 6-8 people
Cooking time: 25 minutes
Best with: Chutney

CHUTNEY
1 medium tomato
¼ habanero pepper
1 tablespoon salt
½ medium onion
3 cloves garlic

STEP: Add all ingredients in a blender and blend until the consistency is smooth. Remove in a bowl and serve with dish.

Note: The amount of habanero pepper required may depend on the individual's preference.
½ habanero pepper = mild
1 habanero pepper = medium
2 habanero pepper = suicide

STEWED POTATOES & MACKEREL

5 medium potatoes
Salt & black pepper to taste
1 teaspoon parsley flakes (or fresh)
1 green onion, chopped
1 medium onion, chopped
2 tablespoons cooking oil
1 medium tomato, sliced
1-8 oz. can mackerel in tomato sauce
1 habanero pepper, chopped

STEPS:

1. Peel & thinly slice potatoes and set aside.
2. Heat cooking oil in a medium sized frying pan, on high heat.
3. Add the onion, green onion and habanero and cook until caramelized.
4. Add potatoes, salt, black pepper, parsley flakes and cook on medium heat for approximately 15 minutes or until potatoes are cooked.
5. Add the sliced tomatoes and cook for another five minutes.
6. Add the mackerel and let simmer for and additional five minutes.
7. Let cool for five minutes then serve!

Serve: Hot or Cold
Portion: 4-6 people
Cooking time: 25 minutes
Best with: Plain rice or Roti

Note: The amount of habanero pepper required may depend on the individual's preference.
½ habanero pepper = mild
1 habanero pepper = medium
2 habanero pepper = suicide

STEWED SALMON

2-8 oz. can salmon
Salt & black pepper to taste
1 teaspoon parsley flakes (or fresh)
1 green onion, chopped
1 medium onion, chopped
2 tablespoons cooking oil
2 medium tomatoes
1 habanero pepper, chopped

STEPS:
1. Heat cooking oil in a medium sized frying pan, on high heat.
2. Add the onion, green onion and habanero and cook until caramelized.
3. Add the sliced tomatoes and cook for five minutes.
4. Add the salmon, salt, black pepper, parsley flakes and cook for approximately 10e minutes on medium heat.
5. Let cool and ready to eat!

This incredible dish is my children's favorite. If given the option, they can eat this every morning. I usually cook this on Saturday mornings along with potato roti. In the words of my younger son, Brandon, this is amazing; I can eat it every day!

Serve: Hot or Cold
Portion: 4-6 people
Cooking time: 15 minutes
Best with: Plain rice or Roti

Note: The amount of habanero pepper required may depend on the individual's preference.
½ habanero pepper = mild
1 habanero pepper = medium
2 habanero pepper = suicide

STEWED ZUCCHINI/POTATOES & CHICKEN

4 medium zucchinis

4 medium potatoes

1 boneless chicken breast, cubed (shrimp or beef can be substituted)

Salt and black pepper to taste

2 tablespoons cooking oil

1 green onion, chopped

1 tablespoons white vinegar

1 medium onion, chopped

1 medium tomato

1 habanero pepper, chopped

STEPS:

1. Peel and cut zucchinis into small pieces.
2. Wash chicken with vinegar and water.
3. Drain in colander and set aside.
4. Peel potatoes and cut into thin slices.
5. Heat cooking oil in a medium sized frying pan, on high heat.
6. Add onion, green onion and habanero and cook until caramelized.
7. Add chicken and cook for additional 10 minutes on medium heat.
8. Add zucchini, potatoes, salt and black pepper and cook for 10 minutes, stirring occasionally.
9. Add sliced tomatoes and cook for another 10 minutes or until zucchini and potatoes are cooked to suit you.
10. Let cool and serve on rice or with any roti.

Serve: Hot or Cold

Portion: 4-6 people

Cooking time: 35 minutes

Best with: Plain rice or Roti

Note: The amount of habanero pepper required may depend on the individual's preference.

½ habanero pepper = mild

1 habanero pepper = medium

2 habanero pepper = suicide

SPINACH & SHRIMP

2 pkg. frozen spinach (fresh spinach may be substituted)
Salt and black pepper to taste
1 medium tomato
½ can coconut milk (or frozen)
1 medium onion, chopped
2 cloves garlic, crushed
2 tablespoons cooking oil (olive coil may be substituted)
¼ cup shrimp (chicken or beef may be substituted)
2 tablespoons vinegar
1 habanero pepper, chopped

STEPS:

1. Take out spinach from freezer and place it in refrigerator. If using fresh spinach use two bunches, finely chopped. Make sure to wash the spinach thoroughly!
2. Drain in a colander, and set aside.
3. Cut off the heads and tails and peel the shrimp. If using chicken or beef, cut into bit sized pieces.

4. Wash with vinegar and water.
5. Drain in a colander and set aside.
6. Heat cooking oil in a medium sized pot, on high heat.
7. Add the onion, green onion and habanero and cook until caramelized.
8. Add spinach, salt, black pepper, coconut milk and cook for approximately 15 minutes on medium heat.
9. Add the sliced tomatoes and cook for an additional 15 minutes, until spinach is fully cooked or as you desire. *This is a great way to prepare spinach for your picky eaters. Once they taste this dish, they will not realize that they are eating spinach. Popeye would have loved this dish!*

Serve: Hot or Cold
Portion: 4-6 people
Cooking time: 30 minutes
Best with: Plain rice or Roti

Note: The amount of habanero pepper required may depend on the individual's preference.
½ habanero pepper = mild
1 habanero pepper = medium
2 habanero pepper = suicide

SQUASH & CHICKEN CURRY

1 chicken, cubed (legs or breast can be substituted)

1 medium Guyanese squash (other squash may be substituted)

Salt to taste

2 green onions, chopped

1 medium onion, chopped

2 tablespoons cooking oil

2 tablespoons white vinegar

2 tablespoons curry powder

2 cloves garlic, crushed

3 medium potatoes

Water

1 habanero pepper, chopped

STEPS:

1. Wash meat with vinegar, drain into colander and set aside.
2. Mix the onion, green onion, habanero, and garlic together with curry powder and half cup of water.
3. Heat cooking oil in a medium sized pot, on high heat. Add the curry mixture and cook for about five minutes.
4. Peel and quarter potatoes; peel, remove seeds and cut squash into bite size pieces and set aside.
5. When curry mixture is golden brown not burnt add chicken, potatoes and squash. Cook on medium heat for 10 minutes until, stirring occasionally.
6. Add two cups of water and taste for salt, if more needed then add. Continue to cook on medium heat for approximately 30 minutes.
7. If there is more gravy than you desire let curry boil until water dries down to your likening.

   This dish is also delicious with chicken or shrimp!

Serve: Hot or Cold
Portion: 4-6 people
Cooking time: 40 minutes
Best with: Plain rice or Any Roti

Note: The amount of habanero pepper required may depend on the individual's preference.

½ habanero pepper = mild

1 habanero pepper = medium

2 habanero pepper = suicide

YELLOW SPLIT PEA (DAHL) COOK-UP

½ cup yellow split pea
1 cup basmati rice (any rice will do)
1 medium onion, chopped
2 green onions, chopped
1 lb. stewing beef (can be substituted with cod fish)
Salt and black pepper to taste
1 teaspoon parsley flakes (or fresh)
½ package frozen coconut cream (or coconut milk)
2 carrots (optional)
½ package frozen spinach (option)
1-8oz can chick peas
1-8 oz can kidney beans (optional)
2 tablespoons cooking oil
1 habanero pepper, chopped

STEPS:

1.   Add three cups water to medium sized pot, on high heat.
2.   Wash and add the yellow split peas and rice to pot and cook for 20 minutes on medium heat.
3.   Heat cooking oil in a medium sized frying pan, on high heat. Add the onion, green onion, habanero and cook until caramelized.
5.   Add meat and cook on medium heat for 10 minutes or until meat is brown.
6.   Add contents of frying pan in the pot with the rice and peas.
7.   Add coconut cream, chick peas, kidney beans, spinach, carrots, salt and black pepper. If needed add more water (make sure water is covering all ingredients).
8.   Continue to cook on medium heat for approximately 30 minutes; or until the rice is cooked to your liking. *It is important to stir often!*
9.   Let cool and serve with chutney.

Serve: Hot or Cold
Portion: 8-10 people
Cooking time: 60 minutes
Best with: Chutney

CHUTNEY
1 medium tomato
1 habanero
½ teaspoon salt
½ medium onion
3 cloves garlic

<u>**STEP:**</u> Add all ingredients in blender and blend together until consistency is smooth. Remove in a bowl and serve with dish.

Note: The amount of habanero pepper required may depend on the individual's preference.
½ habanero pepper = mild
1 habanero pepper = medium
2 habanero pepper = suicide

Salda Roti

REMARKABLE ROTIS

DAHL PURI

4 cups all-purpose flour

2 cups yellow split peas

2 tablespoons baking powder

½ cup cooking oil

2 cups water

1 teaspoon salt

1 teaspoon black pepper

1 teaspoon parsley flakes

1 teaspoon dried thyme

1 habanero pepper, crushed

STEPS:

1. Combine flour and baking powder together in a large bowl. Add water and knead until the mixture forms into dough. Cover with a towel and set aside.

2. Wash yellow split peas and boil in medium sized pot with two cups of water, for 20 minutes. *Yellow split peas should be firm not soft.*

3. Drain split peas in a colander and set aside for at least two hours or until split peas are cold.

4. Use a coffee grinder to grind the cooked split peas (*a blender can also be used*). *Do not* add any form of liquid when grinding the split peas. *Split pea filling has to be dry not moist.*

5. Add salt, black pepper, parsley, thyme and habanero and set aside.

6. Cut dough into palm size pieces (should be 10-15 pieces).

7. Flatten out each piece.

8. Add one tablespoon full of grind yellow split peas mixture, and fold dough over evenly. *Make sure the top is completely sealed or else there will be a hole in your roti and peas will make a big mess.*

9. Once all the pieces are filled with peas, it is time to roll out the individual piece (roti).

10. Use a rolling pin to roll out each piece of dough to make it flat and round. *This will have to be done one at a time.*

11. Heat a medium sized frying pan, on high heat.

12. Add flattened (round) roti in the frying pan, cook for 30 seconds and flip roti over.

13. Use a tablespoon to evenly spread one spoonful of oil on each side of the roti.

14. Continue to cook both sides until lightly brown for approximately one minute.
15. Remove from heat and enjoy with any curry of by itself.

Serve: Hot or Cold
Portion: 6-8 people
Cooking time: 30 minutes
Best with: butter, curries, fried vegetables or plain

Note: The amount of habanero pepper required may depend on the individual's preference.
½ habanero pepper = mild
1 habanero pepper = medium
2 habanero pepper = suicide

PARATHA (OIL)

4 cups all-purpose flour
2 tablespoons baking powder
½ cup cooking oil
1½ cup water

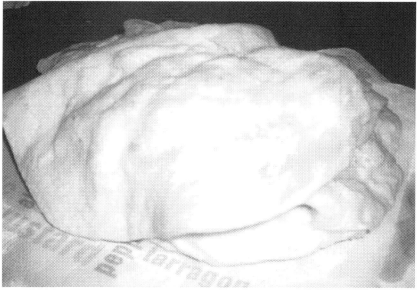

STEPS:

1. Combine flour and baking powder together in a large bowl. Add water and knead until the mixture forms into dough. Cover with a towel and set aside.

2. Divide dough into palm sized pieces (should be 10-15 pieces). Flatten pieces and roll out with rolling pin to form a round shape.

3. Using a tablespoon rub one spoonful of oil onto flattened dough, roll into funnel and tuck top and bottom in (should look like a ball). Allow dough to sit for 15 minutes.

4. Using a rolling pin roll out each ball of dough to make it flat and round (thin). *This will have to be done one at a time.*

5. Heat a medium sized frying pan, on high heat.

6. Add flattened (thin) roti into the frying pan, cook for 30 seconds and flip the roti over.

7. Use a tablespoon to evenly spread one spoonful of oil on each side of the roti.

8. Continue to cook both sides until lightly brown for approximately one minute.

9. Remove from heat and enjoy with any curry of by itself.

Serve: Hot or Cold
Portion: 6-8 people
Cooking time: 30 minutes
Best with: butter, curries, fried vegetables or plain

POTATO ROTI

4 cups all-purpose flour
3 medium potatoes
2 tablespoons baking powder
½ cup cooking oil
1½ cup water
1 tablespoon salt
1 teaspoon black pepper
1 teaspoon parsley flakes
1 habanero pepper, crushed

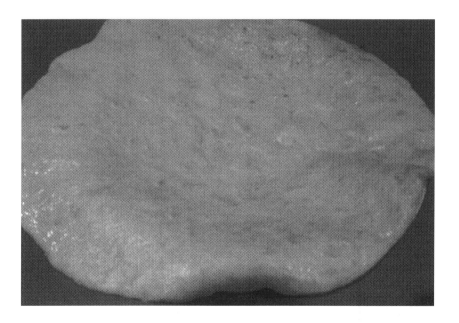

STEPS:

1. Combine flour and baking powder together in a large bowl. Add water and knead until the mixture forms into dough. Cover with a towel and set aside.
2. Heat pot with two cups of water, on high heat.
3. Peel and quarter potatoes.
4. Add into the pot and cook for 15 minutes or until the potatoes are soft.
5. Drain potatoes in a colander.
6. Mash potatoes, add salt, black pepper, parsley flakes, habanero and set aside.

7. Divide dough into palm size pieces (should be 10-15 pieces).
8. Flatten pieces and add one tablespoon full of mashed potato and fold dough over evenly, covering the mashed potatoes (should form a ball).
9. Using a rolling pin roll out each ball of dough to make it flat and round (thin). *This will have to be done one at a time.*
10. Heat a medium sized frying pan, on high heat.
11. Add flattened (thin) roti in the frying pan, cook for 30 seconds and flip the roti over.
12. Use a tablespoon to evenly spread one spoonful of oil on each side of the roti.
13. Continue to cook both sides until lightly brown and approximately one minute.
14. Remove from heat and enjoy with any curry of by itself.

Serve: Hot or Cold
Portion: 6-8 people
Cooking time: 30 minutes
Best with: butter, curries, fried vegetables or plain

Note: The amount of habanero pepper required may depend on the individual's preference.
½ habanero pepper = mild
1 habanero pepper = medium
2 habanero pepper = suicide

SALDA ROTI

4 cups all-purpose flour
2 tablespoons baking powder
1½ cup water

STEPS:

1. Combine flour and baking powder together in a large bowl. Add water and knead until the mixture forms into dough. Cover with a towel and set aside.
2. Divide dough into palm size pieces (should have 10-15 pieces).
3. Smooth pieces into ball shape.
4. Use a rolling pin to roll the balls flat and round.
5. Heat a medium sized frying pan, on medium heat.
6. Add flattened roti in frying pan and cook until roti is firm (approximately one minute on each side).
7. To make the roti swell—immediately from the frying pan place cooked roti in the microwave for approximately 5-10 seconds.
8. Remove and ready to serve!

Serve: Hot or Cold
Portion: 6-8 people
Cooking time: 10 minutes
Best with: butter, curries, fried vegetables or plain

REFRESHING BEVERAGES

GINGER BEER

1 oz. piece of fresh ginger root, peeled and crushed
Peel of medium lime
1/3 cup fresh strained lime juice
6 cups of sugar (more may be needed)
3 ¾ cups of boiling water
1 teaspoon non-active dry yeast
¼ cup lukewarm water

STEPS:

1. Starting one week ahead, combine the ginger, lime peel, lime juice and sugar in a large bowl, and pour boiling water over mixture. Stir until the sugar dissolves completely, let it cool to room temperature.
2. In a small bowl, sprinkle the yeast over lukewarm water. Let stand for three minutes. Stir to dissolve the yeast completely.
3. Place the small bowl in a warm, draft free place for about five minutes, or until the mixture begins to bubble and double in volume.
4. Add the yeast to the ginger mixture and stir.
5. Cover the bowl tightly with foil or plastic wrap, and place it in a warm, draft free place.
6. Let the mixture ferment for a week, stirring every other day.
7. After a week it will be mildly carbonated.
8. Strain the ginger beer through a fine strainer and taste for sugar. If more sugar is required, this is when you can add it.
9. Use a funnel to help pour the liquid into a glass bottle and cork tightly.
10. Let the beer ferment at room temperature for an additional three days.
11. Ready to serve over ice!

This drink is usually served during the holidays with fruit and sponge cakes, but is refreshing anytime!

LIME WATER

12 large limes (juice approximately 3 cups)
6 cups of water
6 cups sugar
Rind of 3 limes

STEPS:

1. In a large pitcher, water, sugar and lime rinds.
2. Stir until the sugar is dissolved.
3. Add the lime juice and stir well. If fresh squeezed limes are used, use a strainer to strain the pulp.
4. Serve at in glass on ice cubes.

This drink is enjoyed on hot Guyanese days. But it is without a doubt the perfect drink for any climate!

MAUBY

1 tablespoon ground mauby bark (can be purchased at West Indian stores)
1 inch cinnamon stick
Orange peel
2 whole cloves
2 cups water
Sugar to taste

STEPS:

1. Soak mauby bark, cinnamon, orange peel, and cloves in 1½ cups of boiling water for 10 minutes.
2. Cool and use a strainer to strain in a large sized pitcher.
3. Add sugar and remaining water, stirring until sugar is dissolved.
4. Half full into clean bottles and tightly seal with lids. Do not full to top because froth develops during fermentation.
5. Let stand at room temperature for two days.
6. Remove froth and serve chilled!
   This drink compliments any dessert!

Serves: Cold
Preparation time: 10 minutes, plus preparation time

MISS MERRY'S DELICIOUS PUNCH

1 – 48 oz. bottle apricot nectar
1 – 48 oz. can pineapple juice
3-6 oz. frozen concentrated limeade
1-2 liter ginger ale
Fresh fruit may be used for garnish

STEPS:
1. Combine all ingredients in punch bowl and serve over ice.
2. Garnish with pineapple or orange slices if desire.

This punch has a lot of memories for me because Miss Merry, one of my co-workers always makes this punch for all of the "girlie" events. It reminds me of good times with my friends. Do not let the simplicity of making this punch fool you. It is without a doubt the most delicious punch I have ever tasted! Thank you Miss Merry for sharing your recipe with me!

Serve: Cold
Portion: 6-8
Preparation time: 10 minutes

PEANUT PUNCH

6-8 ice cubes
2 tablespoons peanut butter (smooth or crunch)
1 cup milk (2% or whole)
2 tablespoons condensed milk (sweetened)
2 tablespoons vanilla ice cream

STEPS:

1. Combine ice cubes, peanut butter, milk, condensed milk and ice cream in a blender and mix until texture is smooth. Enjoy!

This drink is quite simple to make and delicious anytime!

Serve: Cold
Portion: 5
Preparation time: 10 minutes

REFRESHING RUM PUNCH

1-46 oz. can orange juice
1-46 oz. can pineapple juice
1-16 oz. can Coco Lopez
16 oz. Dark Rum (rum can be eliminated)
Grenadine, for added color and flavor
Fresh seasonal fruit for garnish

STEPS:
1. In a medium sized punch bowl, combine all ingredients, except the garnish.
2. Chill or add ice.
3. Decorate the punch bowl with seasonal fruit and serve.

Serve: Cold
Portion: 5
Preparation time: 10 minutes

TAMARIND DRINK

4 quarts water

1 teaspoon ground ginger

2 tablespoons anise

4 sticks cinnamon

4 cups brown sugar

Lemon slices, anise, cinnamon sticks for garnish

STEPS:

1. Place the Tamarind in a large glass bowl.
2. In a medium size pot, add water and boil on medium heat.
3. Remove from heat and pour over tamarind.
4. Let the tamarind soak overnight.
5. Next day, add the ginger anise and cinnamon and let it sit for two hours.
6. Use a strainer to strain in a medium sized pitcher.
7. Sweetened and taste for preferred sweetness, if more sugar is needed add.
8. Refrigerate and chill.
9. Add the lemon and spices (garnishes) just before serving and stir.
10. Enjoy!

Serve: Cold

Portion: 10

Cooking time: 30 minutes, please preparation time

DELICIOUS DESSERTS

AWESOME APRICOT TRIFLE

1 store bought pound cake
2-14 oz. cans apricots
¼ cup sherry
¼ cup custard powder
2 ½ cups milk
3 tablespoons sugar
1tablespoon almond extract
2 teaspoons grated orange rind
1 tablespoon raisins (optional)
2 tablespoons toasted almond slivers

TOPPING:

½ cup whipping cream
1 teaspoon sugar
1 teaspoon vanilla

GARNISH:

2 teaspoons raisins (any fruit can be used)
2 teaspoons toasted almond slivers

STEPS:

1. Line sides of medium sized glass bowl with cake slices (cut about ¼ inch thick).
2. Drain apricots, reserving 1/3 cup juice. Set aside several apricots halves for garnish.
3. Mix juice with sherry, drizzle over cake.
4. In large bowl add custard powder and milk, stirring until smooth.
5. Add the sugar, almond extract, orange rind, raisins and almond slivers (*microwave at high for five minutes*).
6. Gently stir in apricots.
8. Pour over pound cake slices and chill.
9. **Making the topping**: Stir whip cream, sugar and vanilla and spread over trifle.
10. Arrange reserved apricots over top.
11. Sprinkle with raisins and almond slivers.
12. Ready to eat!

This dessert brings back really great memories! My oldest brother made this dessert all the time for us when he was newly married. It reminds me of growing up in Canada and the closeness that I shared with my siblings. Each time he made this dessert it would be better that the first. It is absolutely scrumptious!

Serve: Hot or Cold
Portion: 6-8
Cooking time: 5 minutes, plus preparation time

BREAD & FRUIT PUDDING

6 slices of bread, buttered

2 cups of warm milk

1 cup sugar

2 eggs

2 cups of dried fruit (raisins)

Cinnamon

STEPS:

1. Preheat oven to 325°F.
2. Spread three slices of bread in a medium sized baking dish covering the bottom.
3. Spread the fruit evenly on top of the bread.
4. Beat the eggs, with the sugar.
5. Add the warm milk.
6. Top the fruit on the serving dish with the rest of bread slices. *It must cover all the fruit.*
7. Gently pour the milk and eggs and sugar mixture over the bread. *Ensure the bread does not move.*
8. Sprinkle with the cinnamon on top.
9. Let it stand out for a half hour.
10. Bake at 325°F for 45 minutes, or until it is golden brown on top.
11. Ready to eat!

This dessert is absolutely fabulous when it is served hot with vanilla ice cream!

Serve: Hot or Cold
Portion: 5
Cooking time: 45 minutes, plus preparation time

CARROT & PINEAPPLE CAKE

3 cups self rising flour

2 teaspoons cinnamon

1 ½ cups vegetable oil

2 cups sugar

4 eggs

2 cups grated carrots

1-8 oz. can crushed pineapple (with juice)

1 ½ cups chopped walnuts or pecans

1 teaspoon vanilla

STEPS:

1. Preheat oven to 350°F.
2. Grease two loaf pans and set aside.
3. Stir flour and cinnamon together.
4. Combine oil and sugar in large mixing bowl; beat thoroughly with electric mixer.
5. Add eggs, one at a time, beat well after each addition.
6. Add the cinnamon and flour into egg mixture and mix thoroughly.
7. Stir in remaining ingredients.
8. Spread batter evenly into pans and bake for 30 minutes or until cake spring back when touched.
9. Let cool, completely before frosting.

CREAMY ICING:

1 ½ cup icing sugar

1 package light cream cheese

¼ cup butter, softened

1 teaspoon vanilla

STEP: In a medium sized bowl, combine all ingredients and mix until smooth and fluffy. Frosting is ready to be spread on this delicious cake!

This is one of my favorite cakes and so simple to make. It was one of the first cake that I learned to bake; so you can only imagine, how many sentimental memories are attached to it.

Serve: Hot or Cold
Portion: 5
Cooking time: 40 minutes, plus preparation time

CASSAVA PONE

3 medium cassavas, grated
1fresh coconut, grated (or 1 package shredded coconut)
1 can sweetened condense milk
1 teaspoon black pepper
1 cup butter
½ can evaporated milk (optional)

STEPS:

This recipe is best when fresh grated coconuts and cassavas are used. Fresh coconuts and cassavas can be found at most Supermarkets or any West Indian Stores. I know you are probably thinking so what do I do when I buy the fresh coconut, how do I get it opened? Well it is quite simple, all you have to do is use the back side of a sturdy meat chopper to crack open the coconut. Drain the juice from the coconut and use a knife to get the meat out. Next, use a hand grater to shred the meat of the coconut. This may sound complicated but it really is not that difficult, anyone can do it.

1. Preheat oven to 375°F.
2. Using a blender, blend the coconut and condensed milk together until the texture is smooth.

3. Mix cassava, coconut, butter and black pepper together (*if too dry add milk*). Mixture should be moist *not* runny.
4. Grease pan with cooking spray or Crisco shortening.
5. Spread mixture out evenly into pan and bake at 350°F for 35 minutes.
6. For the last five minutes bake at 375°F to get the top golden brown.
7. Cool and serve!

Serve: Hot or Cold
Portion: 6-8
Cooking time: 40 minutes, plus preparation time

CHOCOLATE CAKE

2 cups all-purpose flour

1 teaspoon baking soda

½ cup butter

½ cup vegetable oil

3 squares unsweetened chocolate

1 cup sugar

2 eggs, beaten

½ cup buttermilk (or regular milk soured with 1-½ tsp vinegar)

1 teaspoon vanilla extract

1 ½ cups chocolate chip

¾ cup sour cream

STEPS:

1. Preheat oven to 350°F.
2. Grease two 8-ince square pans.
3. Line them with waxed paper on the bottom, grease the paper and set them aside.
4. In a small saucepan, combine butter, oil and chocolate.
5. Stir over low heat until chocolate is melted and stir until smooth.
6. Let this mixture cool for 15 minutes.
7. In a large bowl, combine flour, baking soda, sugar, eggs, buttermilk (or soured milk), and vanilla. Stir this with a wooden spoon until completely mixed. *The mixture will be very thick.*
8. Add the cooled chocolate and stir thoroughly.
9. Quickly pour into the prepared baking pans.
10. Bake at 350°F for 30 minutes or until the cake spring back when touched.
11. Cool in pans for five minutes, then turn out onto a rack, peel off the waxed paper, and let cool completely.
12. **Now make the frosting:** Melt the chocolate chips over low heat in a medium saucepan.
13. Remove from heat and stir in the sour cream. Use a wooden spoon to ensure mixture is smooth.
14. Let cool for five minutes. Frosting may need to be refrigerated for a few minutes until it thickens.

15. Spread frosting between the two layers and all over top and sides.
16. Decorate as desire and serve.

For extra moist and even more delicious cake use extra sour cream!

Serve: Hot or Cold
Portion: 6-8
Cooking time: 45 minutes, plus preparation time

COCONUT BUNS

½ lb. butter/margarine (butter is best)
½ lb. raisins
1 ½ cup sugar
3 eggs
½ cup milk (2% or whole)
4 cups all-purpose flour
2 tablespoons baking powder
1 fresh coconut, grated (1 package can be substituted)
1 teaspoon nutmeg
1 teaspoon essence
Maraschino Cherries

STEPS:

1. Preheat oven to 325°F.
2. Use Crisco shortening or cooking spray to grease cookie sheets and set aside.
3. Mix butter/margarine and sugar together. *Batter should be light and fluffy.*
4. Slowly add eggs, raisins, essence, milk and coconut and mix thoroughly.
5. Texture of buns should be firm not soft.
6. Scoop one tablespoon of batter onto greased cookie sheets.
7. Add maraschino cherries on top of scooped batter.
8. Bake at 325°F for approximately 30 minutes or until buns are golden brown.

Great for someone who craves sweet without all the calories!

Serve: Hot or Cold
Portion: 5
Cooking time: 30 minutes, plus preparation time

CUSTARD BLOCKS

2 cans evaporated milk

2 eggs

3 tablespoons custard powder

1 cup sugar

1 teaspoon essence

1 teaspoon nutmeg

STEPS:

1. Pour evaporated milk in medium sized pot and cook on medium heat, stirring constantly.
2. Mix custard powder, eggs, sugar, essence and nutmeg together in a medium sized bowl.
3. Add in pot with the milk and boil for 20 minutes. *It is important to keep stirring the mixture.*
4. Remove from heat and let cool.
5. When it is completely cool, pour mixture into ice trays and freeze.
6. Depending on your freezer setting this will be ready to eat the next day.

   This dessert is my son Brandon's favorite.

Serve: Cold

Portion: 6-8

Cooking time: 30 minutes, plus preparation time

DELECTABLE BIRTHDAY CAKE

2 cups all-purpose flour

1 ¼ cups sugar

4 teaspoons baking powder

1 cup milk

1 teaspoon essence

1 cup sweetened flake coconut

½ teaspoon salt

½ cup shortening

3 eggs

STEPS:

1. Preheat oven to 350°F.
2. Grease two 9-inches round cake pans, dust with flour and set aside.
3. In large mixing bowl, stir together flour, sugar, baking powder and salt.
4. Add milk, shortening and essence.
5. Beat for 1 minute at medium speed or until smooth.
6. Add the coconut.
7. Pour into prepared pans and bake for 35 minutes or until cake spring back when touched.
8. Let cool for five minutes.
9. Remove from pans and let cool completely on racks.
10. Spread chocolate icing between layers and over top.
11. Garnish with coconut.

CHOCOLATE ICING:

2 cups chocolate chips

½ cup milk

1/3 cup cold butter, in bits

STEPS:

1. In small saucepan, melt chocolate chips over low heat, stirring until smooth.
2. Remove from heat; stir in butter, a little at a time, until smooth.
3. Pour into bowl and refrigerate until firm enough to spread—approximately 2 hours.

This cake can be made for all those special people in your lives!

Serve: Hot or Cold
Portion: 5
Cooking time: 45 minutes, plus preparation time

EASY CHEESE CAKE

1 package cream cheese
2 eggs
½ cup sugar
½ teaspoon vanilla/essence
1/3 cup cream (if desired)
1 graham cracker pie crust

STEPS:

1. Beat together cream and sugar together until smooth and fluffy.
2. Add eggs, vanilla and milk if necessary.
3. Pour into pie crust and bake at 350°F for approximately 40 minutes.

This dessert sounds too simple to be delicious but it truly is the most scrumptious cheese cake you will eat. Also, fresh fruit of your choice can be added for even better taste, if that is even possible!

Serve: Hot or Cold
Portion: 6-8
Cooking time: 40 minutes, plus preparation time

FALUDA

1 package straw (agar/agar)
1 cup water
1 can evaporated milk
1 ½ cups sugar
½ cup whole milk
1 teaspoon nutmeg
1 teaspoon vanilla/essence

STEPS:

1. Add water in a medium sized pot and boil straw until melt.
2. Add milk, sugar, nutmeg and essence.
3. Boil on medium heat for 10 minutes.
4. Let cool and refrigerate until it is firm.
5. Ready to serve this delicious Jell-O like dessert.

Food coloring can be added to decorate this dessert according to the festive season.

Serve: Cold
Portion: 6-8
Cooking time: 15 minutes, plus preparation time

FLAN

1 cup white sugar

3 eggs

1-14 oz. can sweetened condensed milk

1-12 oz. can evaporated milk

1 teaspoon vanilla extract

1 teaspoon nutmeg

STEPS:

1. Preheat oven to 350°F.
2. In a medium saucepan over low heat, melt sugar until liquefied and golden in color.
3. Carefully pour hot syrup into a 9-inch round glass baking dish, turning the dish to evenly coat the bottom and sides and set aside.
4. In a large bowl, beat eggs.
5. Add the condensed milk, evaporated milk, vanilla and nutmeg, stirring until smooth.
6. Pour egg mixture into baking dish and cover with aluminum foil.
7. Bake for 60 minutes. Let cool completely.
8. To serve, carefully invert on serving plate with edges when completely cool.

Serve: Cold
Portion: 6-8
Cooking time: 60 minutes

FUDGE (PAYRA)

1 cup whole milk
1 can evaporated milk
1 cup sugar
½ teaspoon essence
½ teaspoon nutmeg
½ teaspoon ginger
½ teaspoon ground spice (optional)
½ teaspoon ground clove (optional)
2 cups powdered milk

STEPS:

1. Add milk and sugar into medium sized pot and let boil on medium heat. Stir constantly.
2. Let cook for approximately 30 minutes, stirring constantly. *Spoon should stand up in mixture.*
3. Spread powdered milk on flat surface.
4. Add the mixture to powdered milk and use hand to knead.
5. When the mixture becomes hard or all the powdered milk is kneaded in the fudge, cut into pieces and spread on cookie sheet.

   The key in making good fudge (payra) is to constantly stir. Once this is done then definitely your fudge will be perfect every time!

Serve: Hot or Cold
Portion: 6-8
Cooking time: 30 minutes, plus preparation time

GULLAB JAMUN

1 cup skimmed milk powder
1/2 cup white flour
2 oz. butter or margarine
1 teaspoon baking powder
2 cups Cooking oil
Milk for mixing

Syrup:

2 cups white sugar
2 cups water
2 drops yellow coloring
6 cardamoms

STEPS:

1. Mix milk powder, flour, baking powder and margarine till mixture looks like breadcrumbs.
2. Knead with milk to form soft dough.
3. Set aside for a few minutes.
4. Form small balls with mixture. *If mixture has hardened, add more milk and knead.*
5. Heat cooking oil in a medium sized frying pan, on medium heat.
6. Gently add gullab jamun to oil and fry a few at a time until complete, and set aside.
7. **Making the Syrup**: In a medium sized pot, boil sugar and two cups of water for five minutes.
8. Add the coloring and cardamoms.
9. Add the fried balls and boil for an additional five minutes.
10. Cover and let stand for six hours without opening. The syrup will seep into the gullab jamun and the result is delicious.

Serve: Hot or Cold
Portion: 20-25
Cooking time: 20 minutes, plus preparation time

GUYANESE FRUIT CAKE

1 lb. raisins

1 lb. pitted prunes

1 lb. currants

1 lb. butter/margarine

1 lb. all-purpose flour

1 teaspoon nutmeg

1 teaspoon essence

2 teaspoon baking powder

12 eggs

2 cups sugar

1 cup walnut (optional)

Maraschino cherries

STEPS:

1. Preheat oven to 325°F.
2. Grease and flour two loaf pans.
3. In a large bow beat sugar and butter/margarine together until light and fluffy.
4. Add the eggs. *Crack open eggs one at a time.*
5. Add the nutmeg, essence, raisons, prunes and currants, stir thoroughly.
6. In a separate medium sized bowl mix flour and baking powder together.
7. Add flour mixture a little at a time to batter, mixing thoroughly.
8. Pour batter in pans.
9. ake for approximately 20 minutes.
10. Add maraschino cherries to top of the cakes.
11. Bake for another 15 minutes or until cake is tested with toothpick and center is cooked.

This dessert is best on holidays such as Thanksgiving/Christmas but can be enjoyed any time!

Serve: Hot or Cold
Portion: 5
Cooking time: 35 minutes, plus preparation time

HALWA (5 POUNDS)

5 lbs. all-purpose flour

1 lb. butter, melted

12 eggs

4 cups sugar

2 cans evaporated milk

1 cup water

1 teaspoon nutmeg

1 teaspoon vanilla/essence

Raisins, maraschino cherries (optional)

STEPS:

1. Melt butter in a medium sized pot on medium heat.
2. Add flour and brown (parch) it on medium heat for 30 minutes or until golden brown. *Stir flour constantly so the bottom is not burnt. Ensure flour is evenly brown.*
3. In a medium sized bowl, beat eggs, milk, water, sugar, vanilla, nutmeg and mix thoroughly.
4. Slowly add wet ingredients into flour; turn heat down to low.
5. St*ir quickly so halwa does not become lumpy.*
6. Add raisins and cherries, stirring thoroughly.
7. Let cool and serve.

This dessert is usually made for religious ceremonies. However it can be enjoyed any time!

Serve: Hot or Cold
Portion: 6-8
Cooking time: 30 minutes, plus preparation time

KANKI

1 fresh grated coconut (1 package shredded)
1 grated pumpkin (must be orange pumpkin)
½ cup margarine/butter
3 cups fine yellow corn flour
2 tablespoons black pepper
2 cups sugar
¼ cup milk

Boiling

STEPS:

The traditional Guyanese way to boil this dessert is in plantain leaves. However, since that is not always easy to obtain, the next best thing to use is aluminum foil. You will need at least 15 pieces of foil to wrap the kanki in. Make sure there is sufficient foil on the sides to fold over batter without leaving any holes.

1. In a medium sized, deep pot, add four cups of water and boil on medium heat.

2. In a large sized bowl, combine coconut, corn flour, pumpkin, margarine, black pepper, sugar, milk and mix thoroughly. *Batter should be firm not hard or runny. If the batter is hard add milk; if it too soft add corn flour.*

3. Scoop one tablespoon of the mixture into a square piece of foil.

4. Wrap (see picture) foil into a square, ensuring all the ends are wrapped tightly (no holes).

5. Gently drop folded foil in the pot of boiling water and cook for approximately 25 minutes.

6. Drain in colander, let cool and serve.

Serve: Hot or Cold
Portion: 10
Cooking time: 25 minutes, plus preparation time

MATHAI-5 POUNDS

5 lbs. all-purpose flour
1 lb. butter
½ lb. ghee (Crisco shortening can be substituted)
1 grated coconut (shredded package can be substituted)
1 tablespoon aniseed
1 tablespoon cardamom
2 tablespoons baking powder
1 cup sugar
1 condensed milk
3 eggs
1 can evaporated milk
1 cup water
2 cups cooking oil

STEPS:

1. In a large bowl, combine flour, coconut, butter, ghee, baking powder, aniseed, cardamom and mix thoroughly.
2. Use a blender to blend condensed milk, carnation milk, water and eggs together.
3. Add the liquid mixture to the flour mixture and knead into a large ball.
4. Use your hand to break dough into four good size balls.
5. Use a rolling pin to roll out dough (flat).
6. Use a butter knife or cookie cutter to cut dough into diamond shapes.
7. Heat two cups of cooking oil in a medium sized deep pot, on high heat.
8. *Oil must be really hot.* Gently drop individual pieces of diamond shaped dough into oil and deep fry until golden brown. *Fry several pieces at one time.*
9. When all the dough has been fried, set it aside.

SYRUP MIXTURE

4 cups sugar
1 cup water
1 teaspoon vanilla
1 teaspoon nutmeg

STEPS:

1. In a medium sized pot, boil water.
2. Add sugar, vanilla and nutmeg until it becomes syrup.
3. Pour over fried dough (methai).
4. Stir quickly so the syrup can evenly dry and form a sugar coat on methai.
5. Cool and serve.

Serve: Hot or Cold
Portion: 10
Cooking time: 45 minutes, plus preparation time

ORANGE PEANUT BUTTER MUFFINS

1 cup orange juice

¾ cup peanut butter

½ cup honey

¼ cup orange marmalade

¼ cup oil

1 egg

2 cups all-purpose flour

1 tablespoon baking powder

1 teaspoon baking soda

½ teaspoon salt

STEPS:

1. Heat oven to 400°F.
2. Use Crisco shortening or cooking spray to grease the muffin pans.
3. In large mixing bowl blend orange juice, peanut butter, honey, marmalade, oil and egg until smooth.
4. In a medium sized bowl, combine flour, baking powder, baking soda and salt.
5. Add into the batter.
6. Spoon into r paper lined muffin cups and bake for approximately 25 minutes.
7. Cool on rack and ready to eat!

Really easy to make and great for breakfast!

Serve: Warm or Cold
Portion: 6
Cooking time: 25 minutes, plus preparation time

PEANUTTY OATMEAL COOKIES

1 cup peanut butter
1 cup butter/margarine
1 cup sugar
1 cup lightly packed brown sugar
2 eggs
2 teaspoons vanilla
2 cups rolled oats
2 cups all-purpose flour
1 teaspoon baking soda

STEPS:

1. Preheat oven to 350°F.
2. Use Crisco shortening or cooking spray to grease cookie sheets.
3. In a medium sized bowl, cream together peanut butter, butter, sugar, brown sugar, eggs and vanilla until light and fluffy.
4. In a separate bowl, combine oats, flour and baking soda.
5. Add into peanut butter mixture.
6. Use a tablespoon to spoon batter onto cookie sheets.
7. Bake at for twelve minutes, or until lightly browned.
8. Cool and eat!

This is a simple and healthy way to enjoy cookies!

Serve: Hot or Cold
Portion: 5
Cooking time: 45 minutes, plus preparation time

PINE TARTS/TURNOVERS
CRUST
1 lb. butter/margarine

3 lbs. all-purpose flour

½ cup *ice cold* water

STEPS:
1. In a large sized bowl, combine flour and butter.
2. Knead with cold water.
3. Wrap dough in wax paper and refrigerate three hours.

FILLING
2-8 oz. cans crushed pineapple (with juice)

2 cups sugar

1 teaspoon nutmeg

1 teaspoon vanilla

1 egg yolk

STEPS:
1. Preheat oven to 350°F.
2. Use Crisco shortening or cooking spray to grease cookie sheets.
3. In a medium sized pot add pineapple with juice, sugar, vanilla, nutmeg and boil on medium heat for about 20 minutes for until liquid is gone. *This will be the jam filling for the pastry.*
4. Removed dough from refrigerator and cut into small balls.
5. Use a rolling pin to roll out (flatten) balls.
6. Fill flattened dough with pineapple filling and turn edges in to form a triangle shape.
7. Gently press the edges with a fork to ensure dough stays closed while baking.
8. Beat one egg yolk and lightly brush on top of pastry.
9. Bake for 20 minutes or until golden brown.
10. Let cool and serve.

Serve: Hot or Cold

Portion: 6-8

Cooking time: 45 minutes, plus preparation time

RASMALAI

2 lb. Ricotta cheese
1-8 oz. half/half cream
3 cups sugar
2 teaspoons nutmeg
2 tablespoons ginger (fresh grated ginger is best)
2 tablespoon vanilla
Almond slivers and pistachios

STEPS:

1. Preheat oven to 325°F.
2. In a large sized bowl, mix ricotta cheese, sugar, nutmeg, ginger and vanilla.
3. Spread out mixture in a large sized baking dish and bake for 30 minutes.
4. In a medium sized pot, add cream, two tablespoons of sugar and boil on low heat.
5. Let the cheese mixture cool.
6. Use a butter knife to cut into squares and pour cream over.
7. Garnish with almond slivers and pistachios.
8. Chill and serve.

This dessert is a family favorite! Any time we have family gatherings, my siblings would request this dessert. So, it is safe to say that this dessert helped my family through many stressful and joyful occasions.

Serve: Cold
Portion: 6-8
Cooking time: 40 minutes, plus preparation time

SALARA

For Dough: For Filling:

1 package dry yeast 1 ½ cups finely grated fresh coconut

1 teaspoon sugar ¾ cup sugar

¼ cup warm water 1 teaspoon cinnamon

3 cups all-purpose flour 1 teaspoon vanilla

1 teaspoon mixed spice or pumpkin pie spice 5 drops strawberry (red) food coloring

¾ cup milk

1 tablespoon Crisco shortening

1 egg, beaten

½ cup sugar

1 egg white, lightly beaten

Sugar for sprinkling (red)

STEPS:

For Dough:

1. In a small bowl dissolve yeast and one teaspoon sugar in warm water and let stand about 10 minutes.
2. Sift flour and spice into a large bowl.
3. In medium sized pot on medium heat warm milk and mix in melted shortening, and leave to cool.
4. Add beaten egg and half cup sugar.
5. Add milk mixture and yeast mixture to dry ingredients and knead lightly to form smooth dough.
6. Place in a very large greased bowl and let rise in a warm place until doubled in size, approximately one hour.

For Filling:

1. Combine all filling ingredients in a medium sized bowl and mix well. Let stand 40 minutes, then stir again.
3. Preheat oven to 375 °F.
4. Use Crisco shortening or cooking spray to grease cookie sheets.
5. Transfer dough to floured surface and divide into 12 equal parts.
6. Gently roll out each piece into a 4-inch square.
7. Spoon three teaspoons filling into the middle.
8. Fold in half; moisten edges with a little water, and seal.

9. Arrange on the prepared cookie sheet, spacing buns at least two inches apart.
10. Cover loosely with towel and let rise until doubled.
11. Brush the rolls with beaten egg white.
12. Bake for 25 minutes.

Serve: Hot or Cold
Portion: 6-8
Cooking time: 25 minutes, plus preparation time

SPONGE CAKE

3 dozen eggs
3 lbs. butter
3 lbs. all-purpose flour
3 lbs. cups sugar
2 tablespoons baking powder
1 tablespoon orange rind
1 teaspoon essence
1 teaspoon nutmeg
½ cup maraschino cherries (optional)

STEPS:

1. Preheat oven to 375°F.
2. Use Crisco shortening or cooking spray to grease and flour 4 loaf pans.
3. In a large size bowl, mix flour, sugar and butter together. *A hand mixer may be needed to ensure that the mixture is light and fluffy.*
4. Add eggs (one at a time) and mix thoroughly. Repeat this until eggs are done.
5. Add essence, nutmeg and orange rind and mix thoroughly.
6. If batter is too dry add milk.
7. Pour batter evenly into pans and bake for 30 minutes.
8. After 10 minutes sprinkle cherries on top and continue to bake. *Use a toothpick to test the cake in the middle to make sure it is cooked.*

This cake is the Guyanese version of the pound cake. The secret to perfect sponge cake is to make sure that the butter and sugar are mixed as fluffy as possible.

Serve: Hot or Cold
Portion: 6-8
Cooking time: 30 minutes, plus preparation time

SWEET RICE/PUDDING

3 cups milk

2 cups heavy cream

½ cup long-grain rice

1 cup sugar

¼ cup raisin (optional)

2 teaspoon vanilla

1 teaspoon cinnamon

STEPS:

1. In a medium saucepan, heat milk, heavy cream, rice, sugar, raisins and vanilla. Stir well.
2. Cover and bring to a boil on medium heat. Let simmer for 30 minutes, stirring constantly.
3. If the rice is not completely boiled then cook for another 15 minutes.
4. Let cool, until it is completely cold.
5. In a medium sized bowl, whisk half cup of heavy cream, to do whipped cream.
6. Fold cream into the rice pudding and garnish with cinnamon.
7. Put into dessert dish and enjoy!

Serve: Hot or Cold

Portion: 6-8

Cooking time: 45 minutes, plus preparation time

THE BEST COCONUT CAKE EVER!

1 white cake mix

1 large box instant vanilla pudding

1 jar maraschino cherries

1 package shredded coconut

1-8 oz. can crushed pineapple

1 cup sugar

1 tub cool whip

STEPS:

1. Bake cake according to instructions on the box.
2. Make pudding according to instructions on the box.
3. Drain cherries and dry on paper towel.
4. In a medium size pot empty the can of pineapple and heat on low.
5. Add sugar until dissolved.
6. Using a knife poke a hole in the top of the cake when it is done baking.
7. Pour the pineapple mixture over cake.
8. Let the cake cool, completely.
9. Top the cake with the prepared vanilla pudding.
10. Sprinkle half of the coconut on top of the pudding.
11. Next, top the pudding with cool whip and end off with the remaining coconut.
12. Finally, spread the cherries on top.
13. Refrigerate for one hour. Ready to serve.

This easy and delicious coconut cake is absolutely scrumptious!

Serve: Hot or Cold
Portion: 6-8
Cooking time: 45 minutes, plus preparation time

VERMICELLI CAKE

1 package vermicelli noodles

½ can evaporated milk (optional)

4 tablespoons sugar

1 cup water

2 eggs

1 can sweetened condense milk

1 teaspoon nutmeg

1 teaspoon essence

½ cup butter/margarine

STEPS:

1. In a medium size pot fry vermicelli with butter until golden brown on medium heat.
2. Add one cup water, stir and cook for 20 minutes.
3. Add milk, condensed milk, nutmeg, essence, and continue to cook on medium heat for 15 minutes. *If you desire to eat vermicelli as a cereal, only then should evaporated milk be added (see picture on back cover).*
4. In small bowl beat eggs and sugar, mixing thoroughly.
5. Quickly stir eggs and sugar mixture into the vermicelli and cook for five minutes on low heat. *Make sure you stir the egg in quickly so there are no lumpy eggs.*
6. Remove from heat to cool before serving.

This dessert can be made into a cereal and serve as breakfast; just add extra milk.

Serve: Hot or Cold
Portion: 6-8
Cooking time: 45 minutes, plus preparation time